UNHCR SA: IT Project Improvement

Mathew

CHAPTER 1: INTRODUCTION

1.1 INTRODUCTION

The background to the study introduces the chapter by providing the context within which the research is based on. The context is around Information Technology (IT) projects and failure as well as what has been done thus far to contain the failure. The United Nations agency, the United Nations High Commissioner for Refugees (UNHCR) in South Africa, the setting of the project of interest to the study, is also presented. Against this background, the research questions, objectives, problem statement and aim are derived before the chapter ends with presenting the structure of the research.

1.2 BACKGROUND TO THE STUDY

This section provides the context of the research from which the research problem statement, questions, aim and objectives are derived from.

1.2.1 Information Technology (IT) Projects Failure

The success rate of projects, in general, has been a major concern for so many years in the project management field and has been covered extensively in the project management literature in a bid to find solution(Cooper and Kleinschmidt, 1987; Freeman and Beale, 1992; Cooke-Davies, 2002; Duy Nguyen, Ogunlana and Thi Xuan Lan, 2004). However, and in particular, the real alarm has been raised in the IT project management subfield where projects continue to fail (Al-Ahmad, Al-Fagih, Khanfar, Alsamara, Abuleil and Abu-Salem, 2009; Whitney and Daniels, 2013). IT refers to the use of a combination of computer hardware and software designed to handle information related to among other examples, payroll, personnel records, sales orders and, inventory control. The use of IT is ubiquitous and is found across the board in all industries (Yeo, 2002). Some of the other terms used to refer to Information Technology include Information Systems (IS) and Information and Communication technology (ICT) and while there are subtle differences, for the purposes of this research these terms will be used interchangeably.

The Standish Group report on IT projects for the period 2011 – 2015 found out that about 71% of projects either failed or were challenged (Standish Group, 2016). A failed project according to Standish Group (2016) is one which is cancelled during the course of the project. A challenged project is completed but over the budget, over the schedule and not according to specifications. Whitney and Daniels (2013), classifies project failure according to the failure to complete the project on time, on budget and provision of expected project scope. These characteristics of IT project failure has been captured into four broad categories by (Lyytinen and Hirschheim, 1988; Nawaz, Kundi and Shah, 2007):

- Correspondence Failure: Failure to meet system design objectives.
- Process Failure: Project cannot be developed within the budget allocated.
- Expectation Failure: Failure to meet Stakeholder's requirements.
- Interaction Failure: Issues to do with frequency of use, user attitude and satisfaction. Frequency of use does not reflect system usage but can be out of necessity and not to increase task performance.

While correspondence failure looks at the technical side of the project and process and expectation failure looks at the budget and stakeholder feedback respectively, they all do not look failure from the perspective of the user. IT system users are crucial because, "however good the software development process, if the users, for whatever reason, did not like an IS they might resist and cause an interaction failure" (Currie and Galliers, 1999:288). This is what Taherdoost and Keshavarzsaleh (2015:84) refers to as the "User risks considering lack of user involvement during system development or favorable attitude of users toward new system".

It is therefore this Interaction Failure that is of interest to this research, how the people, end users of the systems, perceive the system to avoid project failure. A clear distinction in literature is recognized between project success and project management success. Where Project success is measured by the ability to deliver on project goals and objectives (De Wit, 1988; Munns and Bjeirmi, 1996; Cooke-Davies, 2002). On the other hand project management success or failure is a function of time, cost and quality (Baccarini, 1999; Duy Nguyen *et al.*, 2004). It is interesting to note that in terms of IT projects they fail to achieve both project success and project management success (Standish Group, 2016; PMI, 2017).

There seems, however, to be consensus in the IT project management literature that absolves technical incompetence on the part of IT engineers and technicians as a cause for failure but points more towards the soft side (Al-Ahmad *et al.*, 2009; Whitney and Daniels, 2013). Indeed, neglecting social issues and giving prominence to hard technical competencies also contribute to projects failure in general other than IT projects only (Kotter, 1997). Furthermore, prior studies have attempted to identify causes of project failure and come up with various ways to avoid failure most of them focusing on the hard factors of time, cost and quality, however, the social side of the project is also gaining traction (Cooke-Davies, 2002). Some of the important soft factors and competencies cited in prior studies in regards to IT project management include: leadership skills, communication skills, Senior management involvement, Better requirement gathering (Whitney and Daniels, 2013). Poor change management skills in projects is ranked as the 6th contributor of projects failure with 28% (PMI, 2017). This is a new phenomenon that has attracted a lot of research in literature to understand whether the integration of change management skills into project management will improve the failure rate (Müller and Turner, 2007; Gareis, 2010; Hornstein, 2015; Pollack and Algeo, 2015). Consequently, this forms the central theme of this research.

1.2.2 Integration of Project management and Change Management

Change primarily is about transitioning from the current to a future desired state (Lewin, 1947). Therefore when an organization intends to implement change this is accomplished at two dimensions according to (Creasey, 2019). A structured technical solution to the problem is developed on one hand which is the project management side while on the other dimension is the people side where the solution needs to be sold to the users to ensure ownership and adoption which is referred to as change management (Gareis, 2010; Pollack and Algeo, 2015). Project Management looks primarily at the technical side of the project, the implementation of the project plan through project tools and methodology which sets the timelines, the budget and the scope of the project (Kerzner and Kerzner, 2017). Change Management on the other hand looks at the people side of the project or transformation, where adoption through minimizing of resistance to change by achieving user buy-in and ownership is important (Kotter, 1997; Hornstein, 2015). Project management is championed by a project manager while a change manager is responsible for change management (Creasey, 2019). The relationship between the two is well captured by Gareis (2010), where reference is made to projects as organizations to manage change. This refers to employing projects to implement changes in the organization. The disciplines' share the goal of successful implementation of the project.

Admittedly, the focus in Project management literature has been on the technical side; processes, methodology and tools as the critical success factors (Kerzner and Kerzner, 2017). However, IT projects continue to fail and several studies suggest that there is a social side to the problem. Cooke-Davies (2002:189), suggested that "it is fast becoming accepted wisdom that it is people who deliver projects, not processes or systems". Henrie and Sousa-Posa (2005:5), on the influence of people in projects indicated that a "common theme to project success or failure is the people involved with the project". It is therefore this realization of the importance of people that project managers need to have as part of their competence the ability to manage change in projects (Cicmil, 1999; Hornstein, 2015). However, there seems to be no consensus on the efficacy and methodology to integrate these two management science disciplines to avoid IT project failure. There is a school of thought that regards the two disciplines as complementary while another treat the two bodies of knowledge as premised from totally two different theoretical backgrounds and therefore in conflict and not complimentary (Garfein and Sankaran, 2011; Pollack and Algeo, 2015).

A number of studies have identified the integration of the two as a basis to avoid project failure (Crawford and Nahmias, 2010; Jarocki, 2011; Pollack and Algeo, 2015). This research seeks to investigate how to equip project managers with change management skills to avoid IT project failure. The discipline of change management is a wide topic, equipping the project manager with all change management skills will not be feasible in this research because of the time factor. However, the one area that features prominently between the two disciplines is communication and Lehmann (2010:329) while alluding to the similarities and reasons to integrate the two posited that it "is one of the most popular topics in project and change management and because recent studies discuss innovatively this topic". However, the two disciplines view communication differently. On one hand project managers view communication as primarily concerned with involvement in meetings, presentation of the project, and reporting particularly to sponsors" (Crawford and Nahmias, 2010:408). On the other hand, change managers "use communication primarily to engage stakeholders, sell change, enlist champions, facilitate political diffusion and manage stakeholder expectations". While other factors will be considered, it is therefore primarily the skill of communication borrowed and viewed from a change management perspective which the project manager, in this research, will be equipped with. This ties to the Interaction Failure category of IT project failure above by Lyytinen and Hirschheim (1988) which takes cognizance of the people side of the project; the attitude of the users, user attitude and frequency of use. The research will therefore look to see if equipping a project manager with the change management skill of communication improves the Interaction failure of an IT project by the United Nations High Commissioner for Refugees (UNHCR) called RCEP in Southern Africa.

1.2.3 United Nations High Commissioner for Refugees (UNHCR)

The United Nations High Commissioner for Refugees (UNHCR) is a United Nations Agency established in 1950 to deal with all aspects pertaining to the lives of refugees and protection of their rights (Lodinová, 2016; Jacobsen and Sandvik, 2018). The mandate was later expanded to cater for internally displaced people (IDPs) and stateless people all collectively referred to as Persons of Concern (POCs) (Jacobsen and Sandvik, 2018). It is the responsibility of the organization to provide protection, voluntary repatriation, local integration or resettlement to a third country of these people of concern (Sandvik and Jacobsen, 2016; Jacobsen and Sandvik, 2018). UNHCR is a global non-profit organization which in 2016 employed more than 9,300 staff members working in 128 countries while providing support to more than 65 million refugees and other people of concern (UNHCR, 2016). The refugee convention defines a refugee as "any person who: owing to a well-founded fear of being persecuted for reasons of race, religion, nationality, membership of a particular social group, or political opinion, is outside the country of his nationality, and is unable to, or, owing to such fear, is unwilling to avail himself of the protection of that country". (Cherem, 2016:187). The organization has attracted global attention in the last five years "with the refugee crisis rapidly unfolding in Europe" (Szczepanik, 2016:23). This is mainly as a result of the war in Syria and Iraq (UNHCR, 2016; Jacobsen and Sandvik, 2018). In Southern Africa much of the refugee crisis has been triggered by the war in the Democratic Republic of Congo (DRC) (UNHCR, 2016; 2018). UNHCR is headquartered in Geneva Switzerland but has also other headquarter offices in Copenhagen – Denmark and Budapest - Hungary.

In southern Africa UNHCR has offices in seven countries, namely; Zimbabwe, Zambia, Angola, Malawi, Botswana, Mozambique and South Africa (UNHCR, 2018). These are referred to as country offices. The remainder of the countries in the region Swaziland, Lesotho, Madagascar, Seychelles, Comoros, Mauritius, and Namibia have ongoing projects however UNHCR does not have presence but implement projects through other smaller NGOS referred to as Implementing Partners and theses are supported from the offices in South Africa (UNHCR, 2018). All these offices in the region report to the regional offices located in Pretoria, South Africa referred to as Regional Office South Africa (ROSA) where this researcher is stationed and the location of the project where this research paper is based on. UNHCR employees stationed at ROSA travel frequently to the country offices in the region to provide support including monitoring and evaluation. They are highly mobile and when on the move are still required to collaborate and work in teams with other staff members at headquarters, in the region and those remaining at the regional headquarters in Pretoria. The organizational structure at ROSA is made of five units; Protection, Resettlement, Administration and Programme. It is the staff members from these units who will participate in this research. UNHCR, now and again run IT projects at a global level or regional level to try and augment and improve efficiency to meet the organization's objectives as well as move with global trends (Selin, 2018). Subsequently, the organization is in the process of launching a collaboration IT project called ROSA Cisco Expressway Project (RCEP) to improve collaboration among staff members based at the regional office in Pretoria to allow them to work closely especially when in disparate geographical locations due to the nature of their work (Selin, 2018).

1.2.4 UNHCR ROSA Cisco Expressway Project (RCEP)

The challenge facing UNHCR regional staff members based at the regional headquarters in Pretoria, South Africa is that they are always on the road in different country offices in the region away from the office (Selin, 2018). At the same time, they are expected to collaborate and work in teams to support refugee programs in the region. The main problem this requirement poses is that staff members end up depending on emails and telephones to collaborate (Selin, 2018). Email communication while it goes a long way in bridging the gap does not allow conferencing and is time consuming while telephones have proved to be very costly (Selin, 2018). Cisco Expressway is an IT platform that allows mobile IT users outside the organization's computer network to communicate as if they are within the same IT network and/or even the same building through video, voice, instant messaging (IM) and presence (Behl, Gardiner and Finke, 2016). It therefore allows the users to communicate from any location in the world as long as they have access to the internet which can be through Wi-Fi, 3G or 4G (Behl *et al.*, 2016). This will therefore address the need for the ROSA staff to be able to travel in the region and at the same time collaborate with their colleagues. The project also seeks to address the high telephone costs associated with roaming as a result of the staff members' need to communicate (Selin, 2018). The first phase of the project involved the installation of Cisco Unified Communication manager (CUCM), a form of private branch exchange (PBX), a requirement for Cisco expressway to work since it provides the requisite call processing, signaling and device control, dial plan administration and phone feature administration (Behl *et al.*, 2016). The project as according to Gareis (2010) is regarded as a 1st order change as it is a routine endeavor which does not alter and change the core of the organization.

The project will be implemented by a service provider called EOH Pty who will provide a project engineer, project manager and account manager (Selin, 2018). On the UNHCR side this researcher is the project manager and the head of the IT department is the Project Sponsor. While the objectives and benefits, as stated above, to implement this project from the UNHCR IT department are very good and most importantly while the technical expertise to implement this project from the service provider perspective is guaranteed, the biggest risk facing the project is the likelihood of resistance from the people, end-users, resulting in the non-use of the system (Selin, 2018). When the project was announced to the intended users, the staff members raised serious concerns on the possible blurring or encroachment of office business into their private time away from the office since they could be expected to be reached from anywhere and at any time (Selin, 2018). Moreover, while the office does provide the staff members with limited data bundles on their phones perhaps the extra usage brought by the project will eat away into their savings. Therefore the general consensus from the staff members was that the project while on merit in regards to the collaboration function and cost saving it was not in their best interest and therefore should be rejected (Selin, 2018).

1.3 PROBLEM STATEMENT

The dismal failure rate associated with projects in general and particularly IT endeavors, poses a unique challenge to both academia and practitioners. That the failure in IT projects is not attributable to technical deficiencies only, on the part of IT engineers, has been established in literature but that the causes of failure point more towards social factors related to user resistance affecting the rate of system usage (Al-Ahmad *et al.*, 2009; Whitney and Daniels, 2013). As a result, the growing interest in integrating the hard technical side of project management with a more soft, people-oriented, change management seem to gain traction (Müller and Turner, 2007; Gareis, 2010; Hornstein, 2015; Pollack and Algeo, 2015). In particular, communication as viewed from a change management perspective where it is employed to combat user resistance as a result of a change endeavor needs to be explored (Crawford and Nahmias, 2010). The challenge faced by the RCEP project manager shows a messy and unstructured social problem that can lead to project failure (Selin, 2018). The UNHCR IT project, RCEP, therefore provides an opportunity to explore the employment of communication skill to try and learn how it can bring about consensus and agreement among users of the system to avoid project failure.

The United Nations High Commissioner for Refugees (UNHCR)'s ROSA Cisco Expressway Project (RCEP) project manager, has adequate technical resources competent enough to execute the project, however the threat of social issues around the project makes the possibility of project failure a reality (Selin, 2018). Therefore, as espoused by Crawford and Nahmias (2010); Jarocki (2011); Pollack and Algeo (2015)there is need to integrate project management and change management by equipping the project manager with the soft skills of Communication from change management to avoid project failure. The research problem is therefore;

While the UNHCR RCEP project is well equipped with technical resources to competently implement the project, the social issues around the people side increase the odds of project failure.

1.4 RESEARCH AIM
The research aim is;

To investigate, using Soft Systems Methodology, how equipping the IT Project Manager at the United Nations High Commissioner for Refugees (UNHCR) in Pretoria, South Africa with the Change Management skill of communication can help avoid IT project failure.

1.5 RESEARCH QUESTIONS
1. How to equip the IT project manager at UNHCR with the change management skill of communication to avoid IT project failure?
2. What world views are expressed by the users with regards to the social problem facing the UNHCR RCEP project?
3. What action can be taken to improve UNHCR's problem situation?

1.6 RESEARCH OBJECTIVES
The research objectives the study wishes to explore are;

1. To avoid IT project failure by equipping the IT project manager at UNHCR with the change management skill of communication.
2. To identify the different world views expressed by UNHCR's RCEP Users regarding the social problem facing the project.
3. To discover action that can be taken to improve UNHCR's problem situation.

1.7 STRUCTURE OF RESEARCH REPORT

The report is structured as follows;

Chapter one: Introduction

This chapter introduces the research study. The context of the study is presented where the research problem statement is derived from. The research questions aim and objectives flow from the problem statement.

Chapter two: Literature review

This chapter looks, in depth, at the concept of integrating project and change management relative to the research questions in chapter one and investigates how other authors presented them and their findings.

Chapter three: Research methodology

This chapter presents the research paradigm and philosophy of the researcher in trying to address the research questions.

Chapter four: Findings and Discussion

This chapter discusses the findings from the learning process and attempts to answer the research questions while also linking them to the literature review.

Chapter five: Conclusions and recommendations

The concluding chapter contains the conclusions drawn from the research process. Based on these conclusions, recommendations will be made for further research and/or developments.

1.8 CONCLUSION

The main thrust of the chapter was to provide context within which the study is located but most importantly the research problem, questions and objectives of the research. The United Nations High Commissioner for Refugees (UNHCR)'s IT Manager is presented with a problem situation; the possibility of the RCEP project failing due to non-technical ill-defined social issues surrounding the project. The aim of the study, therefore, is to investigate how equipping the IT project manager with the change management skill of communication can improve the problem situation. The following chapter reviews the literature around this study area to learn the findings of other studies in the same area and how they relate to the aim of this study

CHAPTER 2: LITERATURE REVIEW

2.1 INTRODUCTION

Guided by objectives of the research, this chapter reviews the literature to examine findings of other studies around the same topic. Relevant studies will be reviewed to establish whether IT project failure is a result of technical issues or non-technical problems. If indeed non-technical issues do contribute towards the failure, does integrating the technical side of project and socials side of projects help solve the problem? In the same vein, what skills, therefore, should the project manager require to tackle this problem? It is, therefore, the motivation of this chapter to review the literature and try and see how equipping the IT project manager with soft skills from the change management discipline particularly that of communication can help improve IT project failure.

2.2 THE SOCIAL SIDE OF IT PROJECT FAILURE

The increase in investment into the IT industry continues relentlessly averaging 3.5% annually but at the same time IT projects failure trajectory continue unabated with loses running into billions annually (Stoica and Brouse, 2013) . This is compounded by the increased complexity Nelson (2007) of the business operating environment, dispersion of IT systems developing teams and particularly the inability to perform project retrospectives among other factors Dwivedi, Ravichandran, Williams, Miller, Lal, Antony and Kartik (2013). As a result, research around the topic to try and understand causes of IT projects failure and ultimately boost the success rate are ubiquitous in literature (Sauer, 1993; Ewusi-Mensah and Przasnyski, 1994; Dwivedi *et al.*, 2013; Stoica and Brouse, 2013; Lehtinen, Mäntylä, Vanhanen, Itkonen and Lassenius, 2014). However much of the research on IT projects tend to focus on the critical success factors Pinto and Slevin (1987); De Wit (1988); Cooke-Davies (2002) assuming that by understanding the factors that makes IT projects do well will translate into successful IT projects. As Smiles (1904) opined that humans learn more from failure than success situations, it only makes sense that an investigation into the root causes of IT project failure can provide an opportunity for both researchers and practitioners alike to eliminate those failure factors and begin the road towards running successful projects (Dwivedi *et al.*, 2013). After all the Standish Group (2016) reports that roughly two in every three IT projects end up in failure. Of interest, however, is the analysis of the causes of this failure. Technology accounted for only 4% while on the upper end processes and people accounted for 45% and 43% respectively with the rest as a result of product mistakes (Nelson, 2007). In a research of 42 IT projects, McManus and

Wood-Harper (2007) found out that only 35% of the failures were technical while the remaining 65% was a result of people. It is, therefore, the focus of this section of the research to understand social side of IT projects and the viewpoint from the users of the projects.

Over the years there has been several high-profile IT projects that have failed. Some of the cases to have grabbed global attention include the London Ambulance Service Computer Aided Dispatch (LASCAD) project (Beynon-Davies, 1995). These cases drew a lot of attention not because of the financial loses of £1.1million - £1.5 million which comparatively with other IT projects failure is not that big but because of the consequences on human life attributed to the project. The Wessex Regional Health Authority's RISP project had a financial loss of about £63million, the UK stock Exchange's Taurus settlement system in another British example costing £75-£300 million (Beynon-Davies, 1995). Other cases of IT failure as reported by Nelson (2007) particularly in the United States of America include the Federal Aviation Administration (FAA), 1996, IT project to modernize that nation's air traffic control system leading to a $1.5 billion to $2.6 billion loses. The Internal Revenue Service (IRS) 1999 project to upgrade the agency's IT infrastructure leading to whooping loss of $8billion. The final analysis of these failed projects revealed a number of issues including among others; contractor failure, poor requirement gathering, insufficient risk management and poor stakeholder management (Nelson, 2007). What stands out though is the realization to depart from looking at IT failures from a technological perspective but to adopt a holistic approach particularly putting into consideration the human/people side of the equation (Beynon-Davies, 1999).

Levasseur (2010), compared three studies by Kappelman, McKeeman and Zhang (2006), Keil, Cule, Lyytinen and Schmidt (1998) and Zwikael and Globerson (2006) which all looked at the non-technical factors causing IT project failure. All three studies concluded that support from top management plays a crucial role in avoiding failure of the systems. Studies by Keil *et al.* (1998); Kappelman *et al.* (2006) found the lack of top management support as the main cause while for the study by Zwikael and Globerson (2006) it came second. User commitment which is also referred to as user resistance was ranked the second most important factor by (Keil *et al.*, 1998). These studies are important as they highlight more of the social side of IT projects, an area which was previously neglected but plays a critical role in deciding the success/failure of a project.

McConnell (1996) came up with four broad categories of failure grouped into; People, Process, Product and Technology. Under People, motivation was cited as the single largest contributing factor to productivity. Without the right level of motivation, user resistance creep in leading to anarchy and ultimately termination of the project. Other studies suggest that while there are many causes of IT projects failure, User resistance contributes significantly to the problem (Jiang, Muhanna and Klein, 2000; Kim and Kankanhalli, 2009; Klaus and Blanton, 2010; Ali, Zhou, Miller and Ieromonachou, 2016). While examining the root causes of IT failure, Levasseur (2010: 159) asks the pertinent question, "Are they primarily due to technical problems, or are they rooted in people issues, such as seemingly intractable resistance to change?" Hence the next section looks at this phenomenon of user resistance.

2.3 USER RESISTANCE

As part of the Interaction failure as espoused by Lyytinen and Hirschheim (1988) above, IT projects have long been plagued by failures Yeo (2002); Kim and Kishore (2018) and user resistance has been identified as a salient reason why IT projects fail (Kim and Kankanhalli, 2009). In a study by Jain (2004) investigating using IT as a tool for change, six of the failures were as a result of Users resistance to change. Kim and Kankanhalli (2009) reported that the organization IT toolbox conducted a survey of 375 organization and found out that user resistance was the number one ranked cause for IT failure in large IT projects such as enterprise resource planning (ERP) systems. Indeed, Hill (2003: 1), concluded that user resistance is "at the root of many enterprise software project failures". As such, since IT projects are used as a tool for organizational change, consequently there is a strong relationship between change and resistance. Gravenhorst and Veld (2004) posits that where there is change there is resistance and that the opposite is true.

Kim and Kankanhalli (2009:568), defines User resistance as, "opposition of a user to change associated with a new IS implementation". This is consistent with Klaus and Blanton (2010) who view user resistance as a behavioral manifestation of an opposition to an IT system implementation. Therefore, User resistance is associated with adverse reaction by users opposing the introduction of a new IT system (Markus, 1983; Hirschheim and Newman, 1988; Kim and Kankanhalli, 2009). The common theme in these definitions is the behavioral expression of opposition. Hence for the purposes of this research, User resistance, is treated as the negative reaction to the introduction of a new IT system by the end users of a system leading to the failure of an IT project. The resistance can manifest itself in more overt and obvious fashion such as vocal opposition to the project including sabotage. Equally, it can also reveal itself in a more subtle and covert manner. In both cases the result is to delay or even leads to termination of the project (Lapointe and Rivard, 2005; Ali *et al.*, 2016). Various models have been cited in literature in respect to IT User Resistance. A review of the extant literature by Hirschheim and Newman (1988); Lapointe and Rivard (2005); Klaus and Blanton (2010); Ali *et al.* (2016) on the subject reveals work done by Markus (1983) who came up with three approaches to IT user resistance.

2.3.1 Examining User Resistance

Many studies, Markus (1983); Marakas and Hornik (1996); Martinko, Zmud and Henry (1996), have been conducted to investigate the phenomenon of user resistance. There are, however, three broad categories Lapointe and Rivard (2005); Klaus and Blanton (2010) used to understand user resistance that were first articulated by Markus (1983) and subsequently expanded by others (Markus and Robey, 1988; Jiang *et al.*, 2000; Jasperson, Carte, Saunders, Butler, Croes and Zheng, 2002). The three broad categories as espoused by Markus (1983) are 1) System Oriented; 2) People-Oriented; 3) Interaction-Oriented. This approach by Markus (1983), to review user resistance, is widely cited in user resistance literature, Hirschheim and Newman (1988); Klaus and Blanton (2010); Ali *et al.* (2016) will be used here to examine user resistance.

2.3.1.1 System Oriented

The system-oriented resistance places technology-related factors at the center. These are factors relating to how friendly the system's user interface is, ease of use and performance security (Markus, 1983; Ali *et al.*, 2016). In the same vein if the system is not available when needed, crashes at critical times, or is generally slow to react to commands or reliability of the generated data system is questionable, all these can contribute towards generating a negative view of the system which leads to low usability and ultimately system oriented resistance (Markus, 1983; Hirschheim and Newman, 1988; Klaus and Blanton, 2010; Ali *et al.*, 2016).

Klaus and Blanton (2010: 631), cited the frustrations of a user decrying the introduction of a new system, "If you get to a certain point, you can print it, but then if you do one of two things and then you go to print, it won't print – it's been a nightmare. I hate it. I absolutely hate it". This is a common problem that users encounter with IT systems and can lead to resistance. Provision of technical support and training can help ease some of the resistance of the users

(Klaus and Blanton, 2010). System complexity is also cited as one of the issues that lead to users developing a negative perception about the new system. Again, training and technical support on the new system can mitigate the level of resistance(Klaus and Blanton, 2010).

2.3.1.2 People Oriented

Factors affecting individuals or groups such as background, traits, attitudes and experience towards technology informs user resistance as it pertains to the People oriented approach (Markus, 1983; Jiang *et al.*, 2000; Lapointe and Rivard, 2005; Ali *et al.*, 2016). The user as an individual's internal and external environments directly impact on the level of interaction with the system and level of use. Negative and positive expectancy of the system has an impact on usage of the system. Positive expectancy will lead to high level of user acceptance while negative expectancy will lead to user resistance (Bokhari, 2005). Continued use of an IT system will lead to the users getting accustomed to the system and hence resist introduction of a new system (Markus, 1983; Lapointe and Rivard, 2005; Ali *et al.*, 2016). Kim and Kankanhalli (2009) refers to this as the Status Quo Bias Theory which see users giving preference to maintaining their existing status. The lack of requisite skills to operate the new IT system can also lead to user's resisting the new system (Besson and Rowe, 2001). Training can be incorporated to reduce the level of resistance (Jiang *et al.*, 2000). The quality of the training is also an important factor. Any perceived lack of competence on the part of the trainers, or wrong timing of the training can see users deem the training as a waste of time and thereby creating a negativity around the new technology (Klaus and Blanton, 2010). Therefore, while training forms a critical tool to reduce levels of resistance is should be appropriate to reap the right rewards. Klaus and Blanton (2010), while in agreement with Markus (1983), placed people issues under this theory as organizational issues. Facilitating environment, Communication and Training were the factors under this category. Of note is the communication expectation by the users to be kept abreast of the process to introduce the new technology. Any perceived lack of communication or attempt to conceal information will create a negative perception of the new technology.

2.3.1.3 Interaction Oriented

According to Markus (1983), this theory of resistance is divided into two categories; sociotechnical variant and political variant. The former looks at the users' interaction with the system and division of labor while the later looks at the redistribution of power after the introduction of the new system. Therefore any perceived loss socially by the users as a result of interaction with the system will lead to user resistance (Ali *et al.*, 2016). Jiang *et al.* (2000) brings the concept of uncertainty as a result of the users interacting with the system.

User resistance can also manifest itself as a result of psychological contract between the users and the new technology. Klaus and Blanton (2010), describe a psychological contract "as opposed to a legal contract which can be enforced through a court system, a psychological contract is not legally enforceable since it is the subjective understanding of what an employee believes his employer is obligated to provide". In terms of the introduction of new technology, when a user's expectation of the new system is not met, this violation or breach of contract leads to the user developing negative perception towards the new system leading to resistance. IT literature puts more emphasis on user acceptance Venkatesh, Morris, Davis and Davis (2003) than on user resistance however the focus of this research is on resistance.

2.3.2 Minimizing User Resistance

Several studies in literature Kim and Kankanhalli (2009); Ali *et al.* (2016); Kim and Kishore (2018) have attempted to find strategies to overcome user resistance. Shang (2012); Ali *et al.* (2016) applying the change management model came up with four approaches: Directive, Participative, Supporting and Coercive.

Directive Approach employs managerial authority in the implementation of changes. Training of users and rewarding of good work are used to fight against user resistance (Ali *et al.*, 2016). Supportive Approach relates to the moral aspect of users during the change initiative. Venkatesh *et al.* (2003); Kim and Kankanhalli (2009) discovered that perceived support from the organization in the change process can help reduce user resistance. Also important in this approach is orientation sessions for the users, staff appreciation and participation by the employees (Ali *et al.*, 2016). On the other hand, the Coercive approach refers to the use of force by imposing change on the users. Non-compliance is accompanied by punitive measures such as dismissal or demotions (Ali *et al.*, 2016).

Finally, the Participative approach, involves employees throughout the change management process. Vision sharing, empowering users through training, involving the users in the system development process, sharing of information and opening communication and feedback channels can be used to involve the employees (Mumford and Weir, 1979; Chang, Walters and Wills, 2013; Ali *et al.*, 2016). The participative technique is regarded as the most effective method of handling user resistance through the use of two way communication, information sharing, and consultation (Waddell and Sohal, 1998; Ali *et al.*, 2016). The study by Jiang *et al.* (2000) concurs with the findings and that cited training, orientation sessions and refresher courses as actions that can significantly reduce resistance (Ali *et al.*, 2016). Chang *et al.* (2013), while studying the implementation of cloud competing at a UK university observed 15% increases in user satisfaction as a result of reduced user resistance. Action research through the participation of IT personnel in training and showing the users how to use the system played a big role in reducing user resistance (Ali *et al.*, 2016).

Levasseur (2010), while in agreement of the need to reduce user resistance suggested another perspective to the issue that the, "best way to overcome resistance to change is to involve people affected by it in the change process as early and often as possible". This is central to the conceptual underpinnings of change management and in particular, participatory change where the people should be involved from the onset of the project. It has been established that the application of standard project management principles in organizational changes like IT projects which are complex and non-linear is not adequate Levasseur (2010), therefore adopting some of the change management concepts such as communication and involvement of users from project initiation can assist indeed reduce the failure rate of IT projects.

2.4 INTEGRATION OF PROJECT MANAGEMENT AND CHANGE MANAGEMENT SKILL OF COMMUNICATION

As a result of the increasing complexity of the operating environment organizations are implementing changes more frequently (Gareis, 2010). These organizational changes are recognized as a unique type of project and are being implemented as such (Partington, 1996; Crawford and Nahmias, 2010; Parker, Charlton, Ribeiro and D. Pathak, 2013). For most organizations, "projects are often used to implement a strategy" (Parker *et al.*, 2013:10). The majority of these changes, in recent years, have been driven by IT projects which have a companywide effect. Jurison (2002) acknowledges this growing importance of IT driven organizational changes, "in essence, information systems are becoming powerful instruments for organizational change as evidenced by the widespread adoption of various types of enterprise-wide information systems. Due to the high failure rate of IT projects Sauer (1993); Yeo (2002); Stoica and Brouse (2013); Lehtinen *et al.* (2014), project managers in general and IT project managers in particular are now expected to not only deliver technical solutions but organizational responsibilities that result from the use of the system (Jurison, 2002). This has resulted in several studies investigating the integration of project management and change management disciplines to improve on project failure rate (Crawford and Nahmias, 2010; Lehmann, 2010; Parker *et al.*, 2013; Pollack and Algeo, 2014). However, on one hand, while the two disciplines are used to champion change initiatives there is a wide difference in conceptualities and theoretical background and as a result there is rivalry and even competition between the two (Crawford and Nahmias, 2010; Lehmann, 2010; Parker *et al.*, 2013). On the other hand there is a school of thought that looks at the complimentary relationship between the two disciplines and sees it as an anathema to the project failure (Crawford and Nahmias, 2010; Gareis, 2010; Pollack and Algeo, 2015). The next section looks at the historical and theoretical underpinnings of the two disciplines and see the differences as well as those areas of convergence particularly in terms of the competencies required.

2.4.1 Project Management

The development of traditional Project Management concepts, tools and techniques has conceptual underpinnings derived from system analysis and systems engineering (Yeo, 1993; Crawford, Costello, Pollack and Bentley, 2003). Pollack and Algeo (2015) traces the early development of the project management field as influenced by approaches such as Cybernetics, system engineering, and system analysis. All approaches influenced by hard systems thinking (Urli and Urli, 2000). Project management was predominantly applied in such industries as engineering, construction and aerospace all with a focus on quantitative techniques (Yeo, 2002; Pollack and Algeo, 2015). "The planning tools, the cost estimation, and control techniques, all these different parts of the body of knowledge were dispensed among firms involved in civil and mechanical engineering, architecture, and technology" (Urli and Urli, 2000). Currently, Project management has gained popularity due to the growing complexity of the business environment resulting in organizations shifting away from traditional hierarchical type of management style to a more project-based temporary approach (Jarocki, 2011; Parker *et al.*, 2013).

To fully understand this shift, it is necessary that the definition of project management is established. The Project Management Institute (PMI) defines a project as a " temporary endeavor undertaken to create a unique product, service, or result" (Project Management Institute, 2013:3). Project Management on the other hand is described as the "application of knowledge, skills, tools and techniques to project activities to meet the project requirements" *ibid.* The United Kingdom (UK) government PRINCE2 project management methodology defines a project as a "management environment that is created for the purpose of delivering one or more business products according to a specified business case" (OGC: Office of Government Commerce, 2009: 21). Nicholas and Steyn (2012: 4), lists down some of the common themes derived from these definitions.

- A project is implemented for a specific deliverable or result which is in terms of cost, schedule and specifications.
- Every project is unique.
- Projects are temporary and time bound.
- Projects tap skills from multi-functional teams across the organization.
- Every project carries an element of risk and uncertainty.
- A project follows a distinct phase called the project life cycle.

Therefore, projects are temporary endeavors that are unique and are designed to meet specific goals. The leading project management standards PMBoK and PRINCE2 places processes as critical to avoid project failure and ensure success (Parker *et al.*, 2013). PMBoK refers to five processes groups with each process outlining the inputs, outputs, tools and techniques to be used in a project. The process groups are, Initiating, Planning, Executing, Monitoring & Controlling and Closing (Project Management Institute, 2013). PRINCE2 is a methodology and refers to eight process which are used to manage the project. The eight processes are starting up a project, initiating a project, planning, directing a project, managing a state boundary, controlling a stage, managing project delivery and closing a project (OGC: Office of Government Commerce, 2009). The main objective of project management, therefore, is to move from a current undesired state to a future desirable state (Gareis, 2010; Leeman, 2014).

The individual tasked with, "the overall responsibility to plan, direct, and integrate the efforts of all project stakeholders to achieve the project goal", is called a Project Manager (Nicholas and Steyn, 2012:10). It is the fundamental objective of the project manager that the technical objectives of time, cost and performance are met, these are referred to as the triple constraint or iron angle (Nicholas and Steyn, 2012; Project Management Institute, 2013) (Shenhar, Dvir, Levy and Maltz, 2001; Cooke-Davies, 2002). Traditionally failure and/or success of the project is measured against these factors (Pinto and Slevin, 1987; Shenhar *et al.*, 2001; Jurison, 2002). The Standish and Group (2013) referred to a fourth factor, that of client satisfaction, recognizing that the client is ultimately the reason why the project was created (Jurison, 2002). Therefore, if the project result fails to satisfy the client it is deemed a failure. This forms the hard systems worldview that the objectives of the project are well defined and understood (Crawford *et al.*, 2003). However, there are certain skills and competencies that a Project Manager should possess from the onset to help avoid failure.

2.4.1.1 Project Manager Competencies

The Project Management Institute recognizes that in addition to area-specific skills and general management knowhow, the project manager need to be conversant in other competencies for effective project management (Project Management Institute, 2013). The competencies cited include: Leadership, Team building, Motivation, Communication, Influencing, Decision making, Political and cultural awareness, Negotiation, Trust building, Conflict management, and Coaching (Nahmias, 2009; Crawford and Nahmias, 2010; Project Management Institute, 2013). The focus on the technical side of project management and neglecting the social side of projects in the PMBoK draws criticism from Leeman (2014). He posits that projects should be led by change mangers because they understand the social side of the projects better than project managers. At the same time most organizations view employing a change manager as an unnecessary overhead Leeman (2014) one which should be avoided. The next section looks at change management in brief and those skills and competencies expected of the change manager.

2.4.2 Change Management

Nahmias (2009: 2) defines change management as, "the discipline of proactively managing and implementing the changes that people experience within an organization". Moran and Brightman (2000: 66) carries the same theme when defining change management and defines the theme as, "A process of continually renewing organizations direction, structure and capabilities to serve the ever-changing needs of external and internal customers". The central theme across these definitions is the focus on the people side of the change initiative. Unlike Project management whose focus is more on the "hard" side of the change initiative, change management's focus is on the "soft" side. Lewin (1947)'s change management model is renowned for forming the basis of change management. The next section looks at some of the common models of change management in literature.

- The Ten Commandments for executing change

The Ten Commandments for executing change by Kanter, Stein and Jick (1992) posits that the organization needs to examine itself first and see the need for change. When the need for change has been established the second step is to create a common vision and direction for the organization. Kanter *et al.* (1992) stresses the need to divorce, at this stage, the organization from its past to create a sense of urgency. The establishment of strong Leadership and political sponsorship are regarded as very important in this model prior to the development of the implementation plan. The participation of people in the change process is important as well as the creation of enabling structures and communication as the next step. The institutionalization of change is the final step in the model (Kanter *et al.*, 1992; Parker *et al.*, 2013).

- Kotter's Eight-Stage Process for Successful Organizational Transformation

The Eight-Stage Process for Successful Organizational Transformation was proposed by Kotter (1995) as a guide on how organizations should transform. The process commences when a sense of urgency is created. This is achieved by identifying a crises situation or potential crises or perhaps it could be an opportunity (Kotter, 1995; Parker *et al.*, 2013). The second step is to form a team wielding enough power to lead the change effort called the guiding coalition. The creation and subsequent communication of a vision is the next step in the process followed by empowering others to act upon that vision through creating enabling structures for change. Planning and creating visible improvements as short-term wins are critical as the next step followed by consolidating those improvements. The last step is the institutionalization of the new approach (Kotter, 1995; Parker *et al.*, 2013).

- Luecke's Seven Steps

Luecke (2003) proposed the Seven Steps change management model. The first step in the process is the mobilization of energy and commitment through the participation of all in the identification of problems and their solution. To manage competitiveness, a shared vision to organize and manage it is developed. Leadership is at the pinnacle of this model and it advocates for commencing the change process slowly as well as being driven by the top management. As soon as the changes have been achieved, the results should be translated into policies, standard operating procedures and structures. Monitoring of the progress of the change implementation should also be performed.

It therefore can be argued that the common theme among the models is that organizations when performing a change effort utilizes change management but most importantly it is the focus on the "soft" side of projects, the people side (Parker *et al.*, 2013).

2.4.2.1 Concepts underlying Change Management
The concepts in this section looks in summary from the change management models discussed above and come up with the common themes:

- Implementation of Change Management principles from project initiation

Many Organizations implementing new IT systems regards the need to make use of change management principles as an unnecessary cost overhead (Leeman, 2014). As a result, change management principles are only introduced when the project is well underway or sometimes only when things go wrong. This can also be manifested through a small section of the organization coming up with change initiative on behalf of the department which is directly affected by the change. Levasseur (2010) acknowledges this anomaly and proposes the need to take a holistic, system perspective of the change initiative. The fact that people are at the center of the initiative proves the need to embrace and acknowledge that interconnectedness. There is need therefore to involve the people affected from project initiation to ensure their buy-in and sense of ownership of the project. This is as opposed to the top-down, one-way of communication where those directly affected are dictated upon on what to do.

- Ensuring a buy-in from users

This concept captures the one of the crucial principles of change management succinctly, that for the change management process to work users must be involved as much as possible to have their support of the project (Levasseur, 2010). This concept agrees with the first one in that the application of change management principles during project initiation will ensure support of the project. Most importantly this will guard against user resistance a problem change management tries to address.

- Two-Way Communication

An honest two-way communication that involves all the stakeholders involved in a participative dialogue that involves sharing of critical project information and vision brings all the players together. The level of commitment that it brings on all the parties involved ensures their commitment and most importantly reduces the resistance to the project (Levasseur, 2010).

- Meeting Attendance

Participation in project meetings and the subsequent allocation of follow-up actions to the participants does not equal to a tacit agreement with the project objectives. To the contrary, Levasseur (2010), believes that this top-down managerial approach fuels resistance to change. To the contrary, it is those participants that volunteer the own time who are committed to the project.

- Collaboration

Levasseur (2010: 162), aptly summarizes this concept by declaring that, "If you believe in the power of collaboration (aka teamwork, participation, collective effort, cooperation, etc.) to harness the inherent power of groups, then you understand why implementation must begin on day one, why people support what they help create, why two way communication is essential to effective change…". Therefore, Collaboration is at the epicenter of change management, it places the people, the users of the IT systems right at the center of the equation and works to involve them from day one.

2.4.3 Potential impact of Integrating Project and Change Management

As stated above IT projects continue to fail dismally (McManus and Wood-Harper, 2007; Crawford and Nahmias, 2010; Dwivedi *et al.*, 2013; Leeman, 2014; Creasey, 2019). Therefore organizations looking at introducing new IT systems should consider them carefully especially the impact to the organization and its users (Annonymous, 2006). As has been established above, most IT project failures are as a result of the "soft" side of the projects, the people side. Therefore the introduction of these systems should recognize the people side of project which is the change management side of the change initiative as much as the technical project management side (Jepson, 2006; Leeman, 2014). The Prosci group found out that the nonuse of change management in the implementation of IT projects contributes significantly to the high failure rate of IT change projects (Creasey, 2019). "The answer is to use change management principles and processes to address these and related nontechnical reasons for project failure (Levasseur, 2010: 159). Levasseur (2010), found out that when the effectiveness of change management in an IT project is none, the success rate of the project will be around 33%. However, when the effectiveness is increased to 75%, the success rate of the IT project jumps to 83% which gives a 150% improvement in the IT project success rate. However, it is the lack of consensus on how the two disciplines can work together to reduce the failure rate in projects that poses the problem in literature (Crawford and Nahmias, 2010; Jarocki, 2011; Pollack and Algeo, 2015). The lack of agreement in literature between the two disciplines is also found in who should take the lead in these IT change projects between IT project managers and IT change managers as well as the competence and skill set required. While it might not necessarily be who takes the lead but a more collaborative approach between the two is required (Nahmias, 2009; Crawford and Nahmias, 2010; Leeman, 2014). While it is clear from literature that both disciplines are ultimately utilized as organizational change initiatives, it is therefore important to interrogate the similarities and differences inherent in the two approaches and see how the dismal failure rate in IT projects can be improved.

2.4.4 Comparing Project and Change Management

Project management and Change management disciplines are both used to deliver change initiatives in organizations but are based on different structuration and theoretical backgrounds (Lehmann, 2010; Pollack and Algeo, 2015). This theoretical difference might explain the divide and also the rivalry Leeman (2014) on who between project managers and change managers should take a lead in change initiatives based on competency and skills (Nahmias, 2009; Crawford and Nahmias, 2010). This is in agreement with Jarocki (2011: 69) who posits that "project management and change management have been, and in most cases are, sold, practiced, and managed as two almost mutually exclusive project disciplines". Thus, it explains the rivalry and competitive nature between the two disciplines. The focus, however, in most IT change initiatives has been on the technical project management side Yeo (2002), while in respect to change management in recent years there has been a "heightened awareness of the criticality of this discipline, many companies continue to struggle with high levels of IT incidents and problems arising from improperly implemented changes to the production infrastructure" (Annonymous, 2006: 1).

The aim and focus on the two disciplines is different. Leeman (2014) sees project management revolving around a plan governed by events and timelines with the desire to move from a current, undesired state (No installation) to a desired future state where installation is achieved. The focus on the technical side in project management is in agreement with Lehmann (2010) who traces the roots of the discipline in engineering, construction aerospace and other hard sciences (Gustavsson and Hallin, 2014). On the other hand in respect to Change management, Leeman (2014) sees the discipline encapsulated in adoption of new systems. This is the soft side, the people side Crawford and Pollack (2004) of the change initiative as opposed to the technical side seen in Project management with its focus on the project time, cost scope and quality. The main thrust is to ensure non- resistance to the change by the new users but willingly and a sustained adoption of the new order. This concurs to Crawford and Nahmias (2010), who sees the roots of change management in Human resources, Psychology and other social science disciplines.

Nahmias (2009); Crawford and Nahmias (2010) looked at the difference between the two disciplines from the perspective of competence and skill set required to take the lead in a change initiative. They acknowledge, however, that the two are "largely disparate fields that operate within the same organizational territory, that is, the management of change" (Crawford and Nahmias, 2010: 15). They found out that not all project managers are equipped with relevant change management skills to drive meaningful change. They viewed the different types of change based on Levy and Merry (1986); Gareis (2010) 1st and 2nd order changes. To determine which skill should take a lead between the two or combination of both, Crawford and Nahmias (2010), compared the 'behavioral change' required against the 'level of culture and leadership support from the organization'. A guide to decide on the structure for the change management initiative was designed showing the combinations in skill-set required (Nahmias, 2009).

On this guide, Crawford and Nahmias (2010), found out that, on one end of the spectrum where the degree of behavioral change required is low and the level of leadership and culture support is weak requires a Project manager with strong Change management skills or two separate roles of project manager and change manager. On the other end a strong behavioral change is required matched with a weak support from the organizational leadership and culture requires two separate project and change manager. However, when the support culture and leadership is very strong and the degree of behavioral change required is high, Crawford and Nahmias (2010), discovered that the project manager should take a lead but with very strong change management skills. Alternatively, there can be two separate roles for both project manager and change manager.

2.4.4.1 Hard vs Soft systems

As shown above, traditional project management concepts are derived from system analysis and systems engineering Yeo (1993); Crawford *et al.* (2003), underpinned by the assumption that project objectives are clear, well defined and methods of achievement is well understood. In the hard systems paradigm systems are seen, "to relate to functions that can be quantified and controlled, or made more efficient, while organizations are viewed as machine-like structures, populated by essentially predictable and interchangeable people" (Crawford *et al.*, 2003: 444). This, therefore, is a linear and predictable approach to dealing with problems. This hard system approach has, however, in practice been proven to be inadequate when dealing with fuzzy, ill-structured real world problems (Checkland, 1989; Crawford *et al.*, 2003). This is the soft paradigm where people are at the center and the problem is not well defined and methods to deal with the problem are not well understood. To better understand the situation, Crawford *et al.* (2003), advocates engagement with the people qualitatively. This paradigm augurs well with Change Management conceptualization where the people are placed at the center of focus and their different views about the problematic situation are recognized. Crawford *et al.* (2003: 444), goes on further to explain that, "People are seen as individuals, with their own culture and continually developing and refining their views of the real-world situation in which they are taking action. Hence it is unlikely that there will be one 'best' solution". As a result Checkland and Scholes (1999), introduced SSM to deal with non-linear, ill-structured problems as those change management tries to address. SSM has been applied in different areas of project management for example: Project success and pre-project planning; Yeo (1993), risk management; Stewart and Fortune (1995), training and learning; Ramsay, Boardman and Cole (1996) and project definition; Neal (1995). Crawford *et al.* (2003) applied SSM to soft change projects in the public sector and concluded that there are difficulties encountered when applying traditional project management practices in complex environments particularly where change management is involved (Crawford *et al.*, 2003). SSM was found to be very useful in providing a theoretical and model-based approach to learning about the problematic situation.

As a result of the inadequacies of applying standard project management principles on IT change projects, equipping the project manager with some of change management competencies becomes critical. In terms of competencies required for a change manager in charge of a change initiative, Nahmias (2009); Leeman (2014), concluded that communication skills are critical for a successful implementation of IT projects and therefore forms the discussion for the next section.

2.4.5 Communication

Communication is one of the most popular topics in project management and change management (Lehmann, 2010). It is a common topic in both disciplines alongside leadership Gill (2002) which is why it is of special interest for this research. However the two disciplines perspectives on communication is very different. Lehmann (2010) follows the historical view of the two disciplines based on literature where there is a school of thought that consider communication as an important tool of change while the other group see change being driven and synonymous with change management. Viewing communication as identical to or pivotal in change management is a concept that resonates with many authors (Jurison, 2002; Levasseur, 2010; Worsley, 2017). Using communication as a tool of change is in agreement with work done by (Gill, 2002; Anderson and Anderson, 2010).

Change as viewed from the classical school perspective is seen from the lenses Levy and Merry (1986: 5) first order changes which are "minor improvements and adjustments that do not change the system's core and occur as the system naturally grows and develops". These are changes that are transitional and concerned with changes that "are implemented in the context of an organization's existing paradigm or meta-rules (Gareis, 2010: 315). Lehmann (2010) view this order of change as very important and one that shows the human side which entails resistance to change and the need for reassurance. Communication is viewed as a tool of change used by sponsors and leaders of change (Anderson and Anderson, 2010). These leaders use change to share their vision, empower users and convince them (Gill, 2002). Communication is also used, to cope through the transition process Bareil and Savoie (1999) for example during the introduction of a new IT system. This, therefore can be seen to be in agreement with Kotter (1995)'s assertion that change without a good communication strategy is doomed to fail.

On the other hand, change from the perspective of the school of change management places communication as the cradle of change (Lehmann, 2010). Communication is therefore the genesis of change, the starting point and not a tool for change as seen in the classical school but in fact the one that creates change (Axelrod, 1992). These are changes espoused by Levy and Merry (1986) as second order changes which Gareis (2010: 315) describes as involving a "paradigmatic shift" which are " discontinuous, deep structural and cultural change". Thus these are the opposite of 1st order changes which form part of normal operations of the organization. Autissier and Moutot (2003), argues that most practitioners' views early and wide-open communication creating a shared view of the change and hence proving more successful change. In this scenario users are fully engaged and in the change initiative as interactive players. Lehmann (2010: 330) see communication in this school of thought to mean "debate, to dialog, to negotiate to participate". Leeman (2014:3) refers to this type of communication as the ability to "communicate progress and impact on people readiness". This is the 'actual school of change management' which is predominantly 'soft' in approach, as opposed to the 'classical school of change management' which is more 'hard' approach (Lehmann, 2010).

2.4.5.1 Communication in Project Management

Communication from the project management perspective and to most researchers refers to the ability of the project manager to motivate, resolve conflicts and mobilize the project team (Crawford and Nahmias, 2010; Lehmann, 2010). It is the Project Manager's role to "communicate progress and impact on solution deliverables and project goals" (Leeman, 2014:2). In as far as the team members are concerned his role is to motivate and manage cooperation (Project Management Institute, 2013). Communication represents a critical component of the project management system. It entails the communication plan, reporting of the progress of project, dissemination of information and the management of stakeholders (Lehmann, 2010; Project Management Institute, 2013; Kerzner and Kerzner, 2017). Communication as it relates to project management and stakeholders depends on the nature of the project, where at the lower end you have stakeholder-neutral projects up to stakeholder-led projects at the upper end of the continuum. At the lower end the type of communication is more broadcasting while at the upper end it is more participative (Worsley, 2017). This differs with change management where communication should be participative and throughout the project even after project closure. Lehmann (2010), compares the traditional school to the renewal school of project management. These schools show two ends of a continuum as opposed to direct opposites, where on one end, the traditional school, the dominant principles of communication are motivation, conflict resolution, cohesion creation and others. While on the other end of the continuum, the renewal school, the dominant principles are, influence, sharing, negotiating, debate and others.

Therefore communication plays a pivotal role in both project management and change management albeit with a different focus. Sweis (2015), while looking at ranking the factors that lead to IT project failure in Jordan concluded that communication or lack thereof was an important contributor to the failure. The research concluded that adopting a communication plan at the planning stage which addresses not only the internal communication needs of the project team but also other stakeholders to ensure all the parties buy into the project. Equally, Leeman (2014), believes that by acknowledging the different focus of the two disciplines in as far as communication is concerned is the starting point but it is integrating the two which improves the way IT projects are implemented. Lehmann (2010), also espouses the same theme concluding that IT project managers should possess communication skills as seen from project management and communication management.

2.5 DISCUSSION

Given the above, it can be seen that the dismal failure of IT projects continues unabated. This has been a popular topic in literature and continues to be one particularly considering the huge amounts of money invested in the industry. Several factors and sources of IT projects failure has been cited and traditionally technical factors dominated the studies. However, there is a growing realization that while technical challenges do contribute to the problem, the main contributing factors are not only non-technical but are as a result of people. User resistance is a huge problem facing most IT project initiatives resulting in delaying of projects and many being terminated altogether. The users simply resist change. It has also been established that, IT projects are now used as a tool for implementing change by organizations. However, importantly, it has also been established that application of "standard" project management practices in ill-structured, non-linear and complex multi-stakeholder environments where these IT projects are found are in adequate and results in the continued failure trajectory. Soft System Methodology (SSM) was found to provide a theoretical and model-based foundation to learn about a problematical situation and proffer ways to accommodate the different views held by the stakeholders until one they can all live with. The competence of communication from the change management discipline is the focus of this research as the Project manager is equipped with this skill to attempt to learn more about the problematic situation of IT project failure rate. The next chapter provides the rationale behind the use of SSM in this research and how the study will be conducted.

2.6 CONCLUSION

The chapter first established that IT projects failure rate is alarmingly high and has been for years. It was also established that, while technical issues are a source of IT project failure, most of it is caused by non-technical challenges. People, the social side of IT projects, were cited as the main source of the failure. Therefore, based on the above, the review of extant literature, it can be concluded that the application of traditional project management techniques on unstructured, non-linear and complex organization change IT projects is inadequate. The users possess different worldviews about the problematical situation and that not one solution will be the best. The next chapter presents the methodology, SSM, its applicability to this research and attempts to address the research problem and meet the research aim and objectives.

CHAPTER 3: METHODOLOGY

3.1 INTRODUCTION

This chapter aims to present the methodological approach adopted in this research and the rationale thereof. The preceding chapter, in essence, explored the social side of IT projects that leads to failure in as much as technical factors also do contribute towards that failure. User resistance was identified as one of the many causes of that failure. Also, the literature review established the possibility of integrating or equipping the IT project manager with skills from change management particularly that of communication to go around the problem of IT project failure. Finally, the literature review, having established that the issue of user resistance was a problematical situation that can lead to IT project failure, proposed adopting SSM as a means to improve the situation. Consequently, these reflections, led to the adoption of SSM, in this chapter, to help tackle the problematical situation brought about by the likelihood of user resistance to the implementation of UNHCR ROSA Cisco Expressway Project (RCEP). SSM was used to try and investigate whether equipping of the IT Project Manager with the Change Management skill of Communication will help improve the problematical situation of possible user resistance and ultimately project failure. The chapter will present how SSM will be used and followed in an attempt to address the research aim and objectives. As such it is important at this juncture to restate the research objectives and aim as these informs the structure the chapter takes.

Research Aim: To investigate how equipping project managers with the change management skill of communication can help avoid IT project failure.

Research Objectives

1. To avoid IT project failure by equipping the IT project manager at UNHCR with the change management skill of communication.

2. To identify the different world views expressed by UNHCR's RCEP Users regarding the social problem facing the project.

3. To discover action that can be taken to improve UNHCR's problem situation.

3.2 RESEARCH PARADIGM

This section deals with SSM's ontological and epistemological position and associated assumptions. This is premised and located within Blaikie (1993)'s taxonomy and approaches to social enquiry. Blaikie's position on social enquiry is chosen because it proffers an array of philosophical positions as well as providing critiques of alternative positions (Rose, 1997). In as far as SM's ontology position is concerned, Checkland (1981), argues that human beings attach different meanings to the same thing hence the central theme of the Methodology that of 'Weltanschauung'. This, therefore, relates to how people interpret their world not by just by experiencing it (Checkland, 1981; Rose, 1997). The construction of 'relevant systems' in SSM provides different interpretations of the problem situation and therefore consistent with the Interpretative position (Rose, 1997). SSM's 'dividing line' between the 'real world' and the 'systems thinking' world as illustrated in the seven-stage model provides puts this argument into perspective (Checkland, 2000). Participants continuously negotiates and renegotiates in the 'real world' the way they view and interpret the world (Rose, 1997). This is in line with Interpretivism ontology espoused by Blaikie (1993: 96)'s taxonomy of social science, where "human experience is characterized as a process of interpretation rather than sensory, material apprehension of the external physical world, and human behavior depends on how individuals interpret the conditions in which they find themselves in". On the other hand, 'Systems thinking' is presented in SSM as the epistemological divide of the seven-stage model where systems concepts are used for understanding and achieving knowledge of the world (Rose, 1997). In summary of SSM's ontological and epistemological position and associated assumptions "We may regard the ontological status of SSM as lying in an interpretive or socially constructed view of reality, its epistemology as the exploitation of systems constructs to structure learning, and its reasoning strategy as that of model building and testing" (Rose, 1997: 7).

3.2.1 Research Type: Action Research

The traditional way of conducting research predominantly has its roots in the natural sciences (Checkland, 1981). It involves coming up with a hypothesis followed by ways to test it usually experimentally. This approach, however, is difficult to apply to social and human situations which are characterized by ill-structured and fuzzy problems as Peter Checkland discovered over a 30 year study (Checkland and Scholes, 1999; Checkland and Poulter, 2006). Each human situation is unique and most importantly is manifested by different and conflicting 'Weltanschauung' or worldviews (Checkland and Scholes, 1999). Therefore, unlike natural sciences, the different worldviews inherent in social human situations mean the problems and indeed the objectives will be not well defined (Checkland and Scholes, 1999). This is true in this research where the users of RCEP IT system invariably have different views about the system and how it should work or address their problems. SSM, the approach suitable for human situations which takes cognizance of different worldviews was developed using 'Action

Research' (Checkland and Scholes, 1990; Checkland and Holwell, 1998; Checkland and Scholes, 1999; Checkland and Poulter, 2006). This approach was suggested by Lewin (1951) as a result of massive changes socially after the second world war (Baskerville and Wood-Harper, 1996). Coupled with that was the realization by Kurt Lewin that, "real social events could not be studied in a laboratory" (Checkland and Scholes, 1999: A39). Given how social sciences are different from natural sciences, the possibility of the researcher continuing as an outside observer, as is the case in natural sciences, in an ever-changing flux of human situations was found ineffective. Therefore, in action research the researcher "enter a human situation, take part in its activity, and use that experience as the research object" (Checkland and Poulter, 2006: 17). As a result of the researcher assuming the roles of participant, subject and researcher in a continuously changing purposeful human action one of the main challenges with Action research, "arises from the fact that it cannot be wholly planned and directed down particular paths" (Checkland, 1981: 153). Therefore, the researcher must plan to react and adapt as well follow the direction the research will be taking.

It has successfully been used in the field of Information Technology the field in which this research is based on (Checkland and Scholes, 1990; Baskerville and Wood-Harper, 1996; Checkland and Holwell, 1998). However, the biggest question around Action research is how to meet the truth criterion of the research (Checkland, 1981). In the more popular natural science studies, the reliability of the research is measured by 'repeatability' (Checkland, 2000). This means that as long as the findings of the research can be repeated in another study then the findings meet the 'truth criterion' (Checkland, 1981; Checkland and Scholes, 1990). However, in the social phenomena the situation is totally different due to the uniqueness of each research (Checkland and Scholes, 1990; Checkland and Holwell, 1998; Checkland and Poulter, 2006). As a solution to this, the concept of 'recoverability' is used. This means that as long as the SSM user explicitly define the research framework to allow an outsider to 'recover' entire process by understanding exactly how the outcomes were arrived at, means it meets the 'truth criterion'. Therefore, Action Research, in the form of SSM was used to conduct this research. The researcher participated in the study both as a researcher and facilitator as well as a project manager representing UNHCR. While a framework of study was designed, the researcher also, planned to adapt, react and follow the direction the research was going to make sure that the research is 'recoverable' and meets the 'truth criterion'. The methodology, SSM, and how this research was conducted is the subject of the next section.

3.3 METHODOLOGY: SSM

The previous section gave the rationale, briefly, of using action research in the form of SSM in this research. This section defines SSM before looking in detail on the methodology and why it is appropriate for this study. Systems Engineering (SE), as developed by Bell Telephone Company was a successful approach utilized in the field of hard sciences. SE is defined as "a transdisciplinary and integrative approach to enable the successful realization, use, and retirement of engineered systems, using systems principles and concepts, and scientific, technological, and management methods" (INCOSE, 2020: 1). To solve a problem or need, the approach was to define it clearly then engineer or optimize it using various techniques developed in the 1950s and 1960s (Checkland and Scholes, 1990; 1999; Checkland and Poulter, 2006). However, Checkland (1981), was curious to find out if the approach which was successful in the hard sciences could still work in management sciences and therefore set out on a 30 year study to answer the question, "Could this approach perhaps also be applied in management problem situations?" (Checkland and Poulter, 2006: xi). Management situations in this case refer to situations that are messy, unstructured and complex such as the flux of everyday life. The findings of the study were unequivocal in that Systems Engineering (SE) could not be applied to these situations. "It was rapidly found to be poverty-stricken when faced with the complexity of human situations. It was too thin, not rich enough to deal with fizzing social complexity" (Checkland and Poulter, 2006: 18). The SE framework was thus modified and gave birth to SSM. The SE framework, stipulates that "Engineers are basically concerned with designing, modifying, affecting or improving human activity systems" (Yurtseven, 2011: 228). Checkland and Poulter (2006: xi) defines SSM as "an organized way of tackling perceived problematical (social) situations. It is action oriented. It organizes thinking about situations so that action to bring about improvement can be taken".

Problematic human situations are complex as a result of competing and conflicting perceptions about what constitutes the situation based on each person's assumptions, background, beliefs and other factors (Checkland and Scholes, 1999). The technical term used in SSM is the German word 'Weltanschauung' which refers to the different worldviews held by people affected or benefiting from the problematical situation (Checkland and Holwell, 1998; Checkland and Scholes, 1999; Checkland and Poulter, 2006). This is true to the RCEP project stakeholders who hold different worldviews about what the IT system should do and work.

3.3.1 The Suitability of using SSM in this Research

Therefore, the possibility of the RCEP project failing as a result of the users choosing not to use the IT system shows why for senior management in the organization feels that 'something needs to be done about the situation' (Selin, 2018). This situation does not constitute a problem but a problematical human situation which in the same vein does not necessarily mean finding a solution but finding ways to improve the problematical situation. Hence the applicability of SSM in this situation is appropriate. The different worldviews which naturally the users of the RCEP IT system holds about the project shows that there is not one particular view to improve the situation. Therefore, in finding ways to improve the problematical situation, is the need to accommodate the different worldviews and not necessarily build consensus. This at the core of SSM, the need to come up with an improvement that the different stakeholders will be able to 'live with' which in essence is accommodation of inherent different interests (Checkland and Scholes, 1990). It is therefore appropriate that SSM is employed in this research to try and come up with an improvement that not all the users will find as the best but at least will be able to live with.

The different users of the RCEP IT system all act in a purposive manner with the intention of increasing work productivity and, manage to collaborate. It is the intention of all the stakeholders to make changes to the way the project is implemented to ensure that different interests and worldviews borne by the stakeholders are accommodated. These 'users' of SSM whose intention is to bring about this improvement to the problematical situation are referred to as 'Would be Improvers' (Checkland and Scholes, 1990). Therefore, in the case of the RCEP, the users of the system form the 'would be improvers' who embark, in a purposeful manner, to bring about improvement to the possibility of resistance to the implementation of the project.

Finally, it is also appropriate, in this research, to use SSM because of the field, Information Technology, the research is based on. Checkland and Scholes (1990: 53) acknowledges this suitability declaring that, "In recent years there has emerged a particular area of application for SSM to which it is well suited; we refer to its use in the creation of information systems". This proves the maturity of the methodology in the field of Information technology.

Therefore, in summary, the UNHCR IT manager is presented with a problematical situation where the RCEP project might become a failure due to resistance from the users. The different and multiple worldviews held by the users of the IT system means the possibility of coming up with a consensus and solution are slim to none.

The users all work in a purposive manner with intention to improve the situation operating in a coercive environment (Jackson, 2003). The environment of the study can be located within (Jackson, 2003) who defines such environments as, "situations where there is fundamental conflict between stakeholders and the only consensus that can be achieved arises from the exercise of power" (Jackson, 2003: 280). SSM, therefore, provides a learning process of enquiry into the problematical situation that can provide an improved situation that the users can be able to live with. This section focused on the rationale of choosing SSM, the next section looks at how SSM will be used in this research.

3.3.1.1 Credibility, Trustworthiness, Transferability and Bias

As stated above Checkland (1981) used Action Research during the thirty year study to develop SSM. Like Action Research, SSM employs the concept of recoverability Checkland and Scholes (1999); Checkland (2000), which requires the researcher to declare the Framework of ideas, Methodology and the application area (FMA) in advance of the study. This will allow the study to be 'recoverable' during any scrutiny (Checkland, 1981). The declaration of the FMA guards against any possible bias the researcher as the Project manager and participant may have (Checkland, 2000). Therefore, this study used the following FMA:

- F: The researcher's framework of ideas: The researcher's values, beliefs and opinions revolve around the United Nations' values of Integrity and professionalism. Pertaining to the research under study the researcher believes there is need to find ways to improve IT projects failure.
- M: The enquiry methodology: Systems theory forms the basis of the enquiry methodology.
- A: The application area is the IT field in the non-profit sector of the United Nations and particularly the social side of It Projects failure.

3.3.2 SSM Process

Following the establishment, in the previous section, of the rationale behind the adoption of SSM in this research, which is the 'Why' part, this section delves into the 'how' part. This section will elucidate how SSM will be conducted in this research. SSM has since moved from the traditional paradigm of being viewed only as a 7-staged process as illustrated in Figure 3.1.

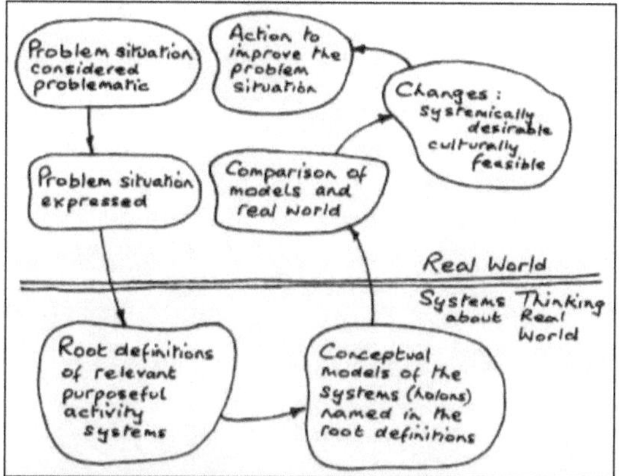

Figure 3.1: SSM's 7-staged Process. (Checkland and Scholes, 1990: 27)

This 7-staged SSM process was viewed as more linear and gave the impression that the process was sequential (Checkland and Scholes, 1999; Checkland and Poulter, 2006). In reality the process was more iterative and could essentially start at any stage (Checkland and Scholes, 1999). As a result of this flaw in the 7-staged process, Checkland and Scholes (1999), introduced a more interactive paradigm which combines what is referred to as a logic-based and cultural stream of analysis as illustrated in Figure 3.2. Equally, the 7-staged process appeared to give more emphasis on the logic-stream of analysis and hence the new representation of the methodology sought to provide equal attention to the two streams (Jackson, 2003).

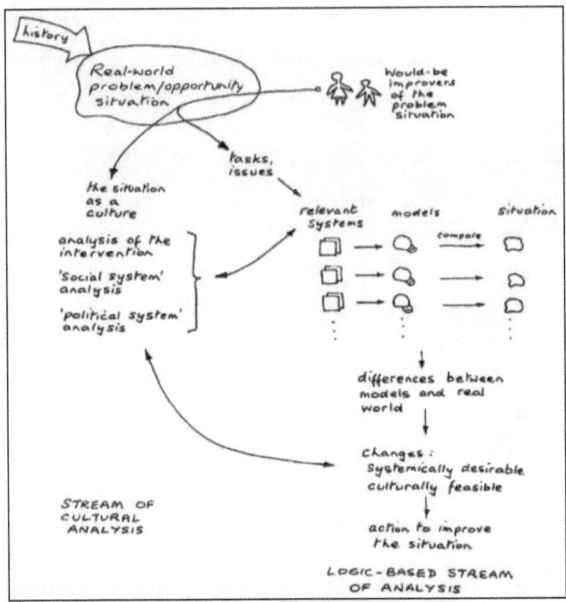

Figure 3.2: SSM's Two Streams of Enquiry. (Checkland and Scholes, 1990: 29)

Simonsen (1994: 8) highlights the difference between the two streams, "The logic-based stream of analysis could be seen as a revised form of the 7 stage SSM, described above, while the stream of cultural analysis could be seen as an addition to the methodology". The logic-based stream uses conceptual models to structure debate and compare with the real world. However, this logic-driven approach while very relevant needs to consider the cultural perspective of the problem situation which makes it a human situation (Checkland and Scholes, 1999; Checkland and Poulter, 2006). Hence the SSM enquiry follows the two interacting streams of enquiry to find ways to improve the problem situation. Thus, the two streams are not independent of each other but rather complement and takes place interactively.

The real-world problem situation in this research is derived from the problem statement stated in Chapter 1. It is an unstructured, ill-defined human situation management at UNHCR find themselves in and feels needs to be improved if failure of the RCEP project is to be avoided. The problematical situation is restated here, *"While the UNHCR RCEP project is well equipped with technical resources to competently implement the project, the social issues around the people side increase the odds of project failure."*. The aim and objective as based on the research objectives and aim is to improve the problematical situation through an enquiry process that allows for the situation to be improved. The history of similar projects in the manner which they were implemented at UNHCR as well as the success and/or failure of those projects will influence the definition of the problematical situation. The actors or investigators, referred by Checkland and Scholes (1999) as 'would-be improvers' of the problematical situation followed the two interacting streams of enquiry, logic-based and cultural streams, to understand the situation and find ways to improve the situation. Checkland and Scholes (1999: 28), describes 'would-be improvers' as consisting "of one or more persons motivated to improve the problem situation". The 'would-be improvers' for this research included this researcher who embarked on a journey to improve the problem situation through a study, while the UNHCR IT manager identified and is concerned about the problem situation thereby instituting the research. The two did not perform the research alone as "SSM is intrinsically a collaborative approach, and sensible 'users' will involve other people in the process of problem handling" (Checkland and Scholes, 1999: 28). Hence the users of the RCEP IT project were involved in the research. In the next section, the logic-based enquiry will be discussed first but it is important to point out that while it might discussed first and while logic is important in the enquiry, equally important and also being done in parallel and in an interacting manner is the culture-based stream of enquiry which will be discussed soon after.

3.3.2.1 The Stream of Logic-Based Enquiry

The original form of SSM process of enquiry followed the traditional seven-staged enquiry as discussed above and as has already been highlighted, the biggest flaw of the process was the impression given that the steps were to be followed sequentially. This form of enquiry will follow a logic-driven approach (Checkland and Scholes, 1999). The procedure to be followed in pursuing the logic-stream of enquiry is selection of relevant systems, naming, modelling and comparing with real-world situations through a workshop where the users of the RCEP project will be invited. This logic driven approach will take cognizant of the cultural stream of enquiry to ensure the two interact in coming up with an improvement of the problem situation.

Selecting Relevant Systems: The research selected the relevant system based on the research questions and objectives as well as either the systems are 'primary-task system' or issue-based systems. The former is based more on the hard system thinking where the human activity system coincides with real world situations (Checkland, 1981; Checkland and Scholes, 1990; Simonsen, 1994). The 'issue-based' on the other hand deals with issues related to the allocation of resources or the flow of information in an organization as an example (Checkland, 1981;

Checkland and Scholes, 1990; Simonsen, 1994). The difference between the two systems is aptly explained by Checkland and Scholes (1990) that, "The distinction between the primary between the primary-task and issue-based relevant systems is not sharp or absolute, rather these are the ends of spectrum. At the extremes, primary task systems map on to institutionalized arrangements; issue-based systems, on the other hand, are relevant to mental processes which are not embodied in formalized real-word arrangements". Therefore, this research took this distinction in cognizance to name the relevant system correctly while at the same time recognizing the choice of the relevant system is inherently subjective.

Naming Relevant Systems: After the selection of the relevant system the research proceeded to name the system which allowed building of the model. This naming of the human activity system is called 'Root Definitions' (RD). "The root definition expresses the core purpose of purposeful activity system. That core is always expressed as a transformation process in which some entity, the 'input' is changed, or transformed, into some new form of that entity, the 'output' (Checkland and Scholes, 1990: 33). Two techniques used in a complementary manner adopted in this research to help define the 'transformation' and come up with the root definitions, namely the PQR formula and the mnemonic CATWOE as shown in figure 3.3.

Customer: Who benefits or is victim of the Transformation

Actors: Who carries out the Transformation?

Transformation: What is changed from input to output?

'Weltanschauung': The Worldview

Owners: Who can stop the transformation?

Environment: What are the constraints outside the system?

Figure 3.3: SSM's CATWOE Mnemonic. (Jackson, 2003: 193)

The PQR formula is an 'input-output transformation process that stands for, "do P, by Q, in order to help achieve R where PQR answer the questions: What? How? and Why?" (Checkland and Poulter, 2006: 39). The use of the PQR as "an input-output transformation is, on its own, too bald to be modelled richly, and root definitions came to be written as sentences elaborating the core transformation", but should be used by considering elements found in the mnemonic CATWOE (Checkland and Scholes, 1990: 35). To make the 'Root Definition' meaningful using CATWOE the pairing of the 'transformation process' (T) and the 'Worldview' (W) is crucial (Checkland and Scholes, 1990). Therefore, this research took this into consideration when naming the root definition but importantly by using the two techniques to come up with a rich 'Root definition'. The next section looks at developing the models that were used to structure debate to find ways to improve the problematic situation.

Modelling Relevant Systems: After coming up with the 'Root Definition' using the PQR formula and the mnemonic CATWOE in the previous section which essentially is a description of the core transformation, this section creates a purposeful 'human activity systems which are the models that were used to structure debate when comparing the models with real situations. Checkland and Scholes (1990: 36), summarizes the procedure followed, "The modelling language is based upon verbs, and the modelling process consists of assembling and structuring the minimum necessary activities to carry out the transformation process in the light of the definitions of the CATWOE elements". Therefore, this means that the modeling is done by following the CATWOE elements to bring about the transformation through a number of activities. A core activity was identified which was contingent upon other activities happening first and altogether these activities should be 7±2 (Checkland and Scholes, 1990; Checkland and Poulter, 2006). The construction of this System or 'holon', Checkland and Scholes (1990), requires a monitoring and control subsystem which measure the success of the transformation process based on three criterion called the 3E's namely: Efficacy – 'does the means work?'; Efficiency – 'amount of output divided by amount of resources used'; Effectiveness – 'Is the transformation meeting the longer term aim?' (Checkland and Scholes, 1990: 39). The judgement of the model can be supplemented by considering two more e's to make them 5 using Ethics and Aesthetics Checkland and Scholes (1990); Checkland and Poulter (2006) but for the purposes of this research only the 3E's will be considered because the research does not have the element of Ethics and Aesthetics as part of the objectives of the research.

This research followed the procedure described above through a workshop where all the users of the RCEP were invited. Naming of the relevant system was done first whether it's a 'primary task' or 'issue-based'. Formulation of the 'Root Definition using CATWOE and PQR formula techniques. Then a model was constructed while a monitoring and control system using the 3E's was used. The workshop is not a Focus group since the facilitator is also a participant and a researcher at the same time. Focus groups require the services of a facilitator and assistant which is not the case with SSM (Casey and Krueger, 1994; Burrows and Kendall, 1997).

Comparing Models with Perceived Reality: Checkland and Scholes (1990: 43) succinctly summarizes the activities to be carried out at this stage that, "Models are only a means to an end, which is to have a well-structured and coherent debate about a problematical situation in order to decide how to improve it". Therefore, the model built in the previous section was used to structure debate in order to improve the problematical situation. There are four ways going about the debate namely; informal discussion, formal questioning, scenario writing based on the models and modeling the real world using the models (Checkland and Scholes, 1990). When the model is used to generate the questions to start the debate this can be carried out through a workshop by a group of people or through one-on-one interviews (Checkland and Poulter, 2006). This comparison of the models built in the previous section will be debated or compared with the real situation in the workshop. The two ways used to perform the comparison between the conceptual model and real-world situation is by using a filling a matrix with pre-determined questions or by hypothetically performing the activities on the model then comparing the resultant scenario with real-world scenario (Checkland and Scholes, 1990; Simonsen, 1994). In this research the second option of notionally operating the model and performing the activities and writing the scenario was used. Because the models created can be practical it will be beneficial for the Users of RCEP IT system to try and perform the activities, albeit notionally, but that assists in generating live debate and coming up with improvement to the problematical situation. It is important, at this juncture, to mention that the main objective of the comparison of the conceptual models and the real-life situation is to find an 'accommodation' among the different worldviews one that all the stakeholders can 'live with' (Checkland and Poulter, 2006). However, this accommodation should be culturally sensitive and this where the 'Cultural-stream of enquiry, the subject of the next section, comes which would be performed in parallel to the logic-stream of enquiry (Checkland and Scholes, 1999).

3.3.2.2 The Stream of Cultural Enquiry

While the stream of logic-based enquiry was performed, in parallel, the stream of cultural enquiry was also being conducted. The stream of cultural enquiry takes cognizance of the fact that, while the facts and logic in the logic-based enquiry is important in human situations, equally important is that the "feel of them, their felt texture , derives equally (or more) from the myths and meanings which human beings attribute to their professional (and personal) entanglements with their fellow beings" (Checkland and Scholes, 1990: 44). Thus, the enquiry into logic and facts requires cultural understanding for any changes to be meaningful. The stream of culturally based enquiry is based on following activities:

- Making rich pictures
- Analysis one – the intervention itself
- Analysis two – Social Analysis
- Analysis three – Political Analysis

Analysis two and three was performed through one-on-one interviews, observation and interaction with the RCEP users, while Analysis one was be performed by the researcher. A semi-structured approach was used to give interviewees freedom to fully express themselves. Due to the sensitivity of the subject area face-to-face interviewing was chosen. This is in line with Abadie, Abbott, Abdullah, Abma, Abravanel, Achilles, Adams, Agle, Alberti and Allison (2015: 494) who posits that one of the main advantages of Semi-structure interviews is, "If you need to conduct a formative program evaluation and want one-on-one interviews with key program managers, staff, and front-line service providers". This study involved interviewing the users of the RCEP project who were key staff to determine the success or failure of the project. Rich pictures was done to diagrammatically present the problem situation.

3.3.2.2.1 Making Rich Pictures

The popular way of presenting a problematical situation was through a linear prose however this has the biggest weakness of the inability to capture the different relationships and interactions (Simonsen, 1994). Checkland and Scholes (1990); Checkland and Poulter (2006) came up with the idea of rich pictures as a way to show in a snap view the multiple interacting relationship. The rich picture is drawn following formal and informal interviews, attending meetings, talking to the affected people and other techniques (Checkland and Scholes, 1990). Of great importance in regards to rich pictures is the fact that, "however rich they are they could be richer, and such pictures record a snapshot of a situation which itself not remain static for long" (Checkland and Poulter, 2006: 27). It is a task therefore which is continuously updated throughout the enquiry process and is not static.

In the same vein and in as far as this research is concerned, formal and informal interviews with the users of the RCEP IT system were conducted to find out about the problematical situation. The researcher also attended meetings with the technical project implementers and senior management to find out their worldview of the problematical situation. This will enable the problem situation to be presented in rich pictures in agreement to what Checkland and Scholes (1999: 183) explained on the use of rich pictures that the "best known is the policy of representing the problem situation itself in the form of so-called 'rich pictures'".

3.3.2.2.2 Analysis One – The Intervention itself

There are three critical roles that fall under this category when finding out about the problematical situation (Checkland and Scholes, 1990; Checkland and Poulter, 2006). These are roles that do not apply to specific people since one person or group could be found in multiple roles. The three roles are:

- Client – The person or group who caused the investigation to be carried out.
- Problem solver or Practitioner – The person or group conducting the investigation and wishes to do something about the problematical situation.
- Problem-owners – are person(s) or stakeholders concerned or affected by the problem situation and outcome of the investigation.

This researcher conducted Analysis one based on the interaction with the project stakeholders particularly with the UNHCR IT manager who requested for the study and came up with the roles as stated above.

3.3.2.2.3 Analysis two – Social Analysis

In this analysis there are three elements that are present according to Checkland and Poulter (2006), to show the social texture of a human situation and these are:

- Roles - Both formal and informal roles within an organization such as Chief executive officers (formal) and Boat-rocker (Informal).
- Norms – Behaviors expected or associated with each role.
- Values – The criterion of judging each role according to behavior.

The 'role' is a social position recognized by the people in the problematical situation as important, this role is accompanied by expected behaviors and the performance of this role will be judged by the local values (Checkland and Scholes, 1990). Analysis Two was conducted, in this research, through formal one-on-one interviews where the three elements were found. The interview schedule is found in Appendix A.

3.3.2.2.4 Analysis Three – Political Analysis

'Finding out' through Analysis three (political) refers to the arrangement of power within that problematical situation and this is related to the choice of conceptual models that will be chosen and ultimately changes that will be deemed 'culturally feasible' at the improvement stage (Checkland and Poulter, 2006).

In this research, informal and formal one-on-one interviews due to the sensitivity of the matter and the need for the users to speak freely were used. Questions that were asked were around how power is obtained, exercised, preserved or passed on in the organization. Also asked is the nature of power that is being held in terms of who has the power to influence distribution of resources, influence others and who can define the needs of the others. The interview schedule is found in Appendix A. Finally, the disposition of power needed to be established within the organization.

3.3.2.3 Making Desirable and Feasible Changes- 'Action to Improve'

The two streams of enquiry discussed above; the logic-based and cultural based stream, "converge on a structured debate concerned with defining changes which would help remove the dissatisfaction" (Checkland and Scholes, 1990: 52). Therefore, this means that after concurrently following the two streams as shown above to structure debate, the next step was the implementation of the changes that can bring about improvement and accommodate the different interests and 'Weltanschauung' of the RCEP stakeholders. The criteria to measure the acceptability of the activities chosen in the final model to bring about the changes is how 'systematically desirable' and 'culturally feasible' they are (Checkland, 1981; Checkland and Scholes, 1990; Checkland and Poulter, 2006). The changes that are a product of the debate brought about by comparing the conceptual models and the real-world situation should be perceived as relevant. While on the other hand the same changes would be perceived meaningful only if they are relevant to that culture and within its worldview (Checkland and Scholes, 1990).

Therefore in this research, the product of the debate to be undertaken by comparing the chosen conceptual model and the real-situation should be deemed 'systematical desirable' as long as they are relevant to the UNHCR RCEP project and the quest to improve the problematical situation of possible project failure. Additionally, the new changes, no matter how small or big, should fit into the culture of UNHCR and its worldview to be deemed meaningful. If the changes are not desirable and culturally feasible then the SSM process starts again (Checkland and Scholes, 1990). Subjectivity is a reality and inherent in the SSM process, as was shown in the section, unlike the natural sciences, repeatability of the results is not found in SSM.

3.4 DATA ANALYSIS

With regards to data analysis, Checkland (2000), uses SSM for model building and regards the models, "not as explanations of reality, merely systems-based constructs to be held up against the perceived world for the purposes of comparison" (Rose, 1997: 10). This is key because it differentiates modelling from theory testing and building which requires sampling and data analysis. Checkland and Poulter (2006) when working in the NHS project the SSM enquiry approach employed was coming up with a model for an evaluation process for the project's change program. The analysis of data requires comparison of the models with the real world (Rose, 1997; Checkland and Scholes, 1999; Jackson, 2003). This is how the data analysis for this study was employed; the collection of data using qualitative methods of semi-structured interviews and observations during the cultural stream of analysis was used simultaneously to build models during the logic stream of analysis. The result which was used to compare with the real world.

3.5 RESEARCH FRAMEWORK

The Research framework provides the structure that the research followed in trying to answer the research questions and meet the research aim and objectives. The research framework for this research is illustrated in Figure 3.4:

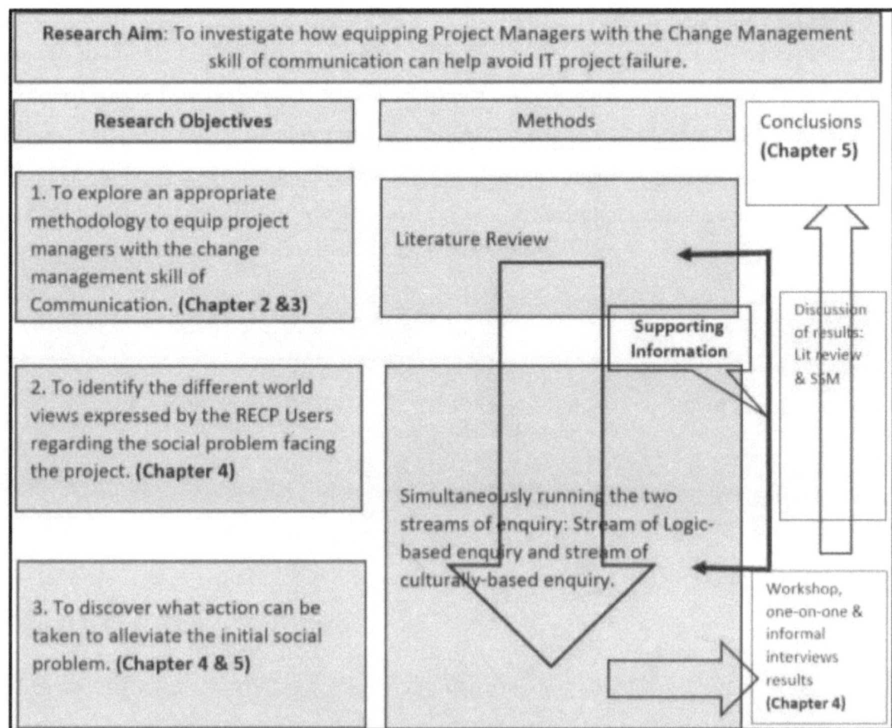

Figure 3.4: Research Framework. (Silva Alvarado, 2016: 47)

The research aim is shown right at the top while the research objectives are on the left most column. The first objective was dealt with in chapter 2 and 3 while chapter 4 dealt with objective 3. The last objective, number three, was presented in chapter 4 and 5. Supporting information is derived from the literature review and SSM process. The workshop results are found in chapter 4 which led to the discussion of the findings and conclusion in chapter 5.

3.6 ETHICAL CONSIDERATIONS

The Soft Systems Methodology requires stakeholder participation and this research was accomplished by hosting a workshop as well as semi-structures interviews with the users of the RCEP IT system. All the users of the system were invited as part of the introduction of the system to the users. Users were formally invited to the workshop through an email. The Supervisor of the Information and Technology (IT) department approved the hosting of the workshop. Research Ethical Clearance was granted by the department.

3.7 CONCLUSION
This chapter presented the research framework for the study based on SSM, a form of Action Research. This framework intends to give an outsider an explicit process on which the research will be done to ensure that the truth criterion of social phenomena such as this one can be recovered. The following chapter followed the SSM process to investigate the problematical situation and 'take action to improve'.

CHAPTER 4: RESULTS AND DISCUSSION

4.1 INTRODUCTION

In Chapter 1 an ill-structured problematical situation was identified, one in which the UNHCR IT Manager felt the RCEP users threatened to resist the RCEP system thereby deeming it a failure. The research aim and objectives were subsequently derived from the identified situation. Chapter 2 reviewed the work done by other authors around user resistance in the field of IT project management and the resultant rate of project failure. The preceding chapter identified SSM as the methodology suitable to perform an investigation into the possible resistance to the project by RCEP users. This chapter, therefore, collates all the foregoing information from the previous chapters into an enquiry process, as set out in the methodology chapter, to find an improvement in the problematical situation.

4.2 BRIEF CONTEXTUAL BACKGROUND

This section briefly revisits the preceding chapters in an attempt to provide context for SSM's enquiry process to follow. The UNHCR IT manager is faced with a problematical situation which threatens the RCEP IT project to be rendered a failure. The users of the RCEP IT project, among other reservations, feel that the project encroaches into their private life and thereby blurring the borders between work hours and personal time. It is for this reason that they appear resistant to the introduction of a new IT system. The literature review established that indeed user resistance to introduction of IT projects is a major cause for project failure. The focus on the 'hard' side of projects and forgetting the 'soft' perspective, where Change Management sits, has also contributed to this situation, it was equally established. Consequently, as a remedial action, it was also recognized, in the same chapter that the integration of the two disciplines, can assist in addressing the problematical situation. It is against this background that the UNHCR IT Manager, assented to this researcher's proposal, who is the Project Manager of the RCEP project, to investigate the problematical situation using SSM with a view to improve the situation. It is the aim of the research, therefore, to learn through the SSM inquiry process by following the logic-based and cultural-based streams of analysis to find an accommodation among the different worldviews exhibited by the stakeholders of the project. The next section follows the methodology set out in the preceding chapter in seeking an improvement in the situation. The stream of cultural of analysis will be conducted first and then the logic-based stream of analysis thereafter before comparing the conceptual model and perceived reality. Finding an improvement that is culturally feasible and systematically desirable will be looked at in the following chapter. It is important, to state that for the purposes of conducting the inquiry process, it appears the two streams of analysis will be done independently, however as mentioned in the preceding chapter, the two are done simultaneously and feeds into each other.

4.3 THE STREAM OF CULTURAL ENQUIRY

As stated previously the stream of cultural enquiry focuses, in part, on the myths and meanings in which human beings attribute to any human situation. The cultural analysis for the RCEP project will be conducted through the following types of enquiry:

- Analysis one – the intervention itself.
- Analysis two – Social analysis.
- Analysis three – Political analysis.

The three types of inquiry will be continuously updated during the entire intervention process and will be incorporated into a rich picture. The stream of cultural analysis findings will feed into the logic-stream of analysis which will be discussed later. The first section looks at Analysis one, the intervention itself.

4.3.1 Analysis One: The Intervention into the RCEP problematical situation

The intervention itself into the RCEP project problematical situation was conducted by identifying the roles of:

- The Client.
- The problem-solver/Practitioner.
- The problem owners/Owners of the issue.

The identification of the three roles relevant to the RCEP project was done through interaction with the UNHCR IT manager and also with the RCEP users. Figure 4.1 illustrates these roles diagrammatically. The clients; the UNHCR IT Manager and this researcher causes the intervention to be carried. The RCEP users, the UNHCR IT Manager and the researcher will come together as 'problem solvers' and conduct the investigation. The 'problem solvers' then identifies the same group as 'problem owners'.

Client:

The UNHCR IT manager, representing the entire UNHCR management, is the one who noticed that success of the RCEP project was under threat and that something needed to be done.

Through the interaction that the researcher had with the IT manager he expressed his desire to see the project succeeding. To him success of the project would see the users' making use of the system as it is designed for. The system was designed to facilitate collaboration among staff members due to nature of their work which involved a lot of travelling. When this researcher offered his services to investigate the problem situation through an inquiry process to find an improvement, he is also a fit as a role client. The researcher for the reason that he suggested SSM as a possible methodology that could be used in the intervention, means he contributed into the research being conducted. To the researcher the expectations of the research is to learn through the iterative inquiry process and hopefully arrive at a position when the different worldviews held by the different stakeholders of the project can be accommodated. This is the point when all the stakeholders can be able to 'live with' the improvements made to the project. Thus, the UNHCR IT Manager occupies the position of role 'Client'.

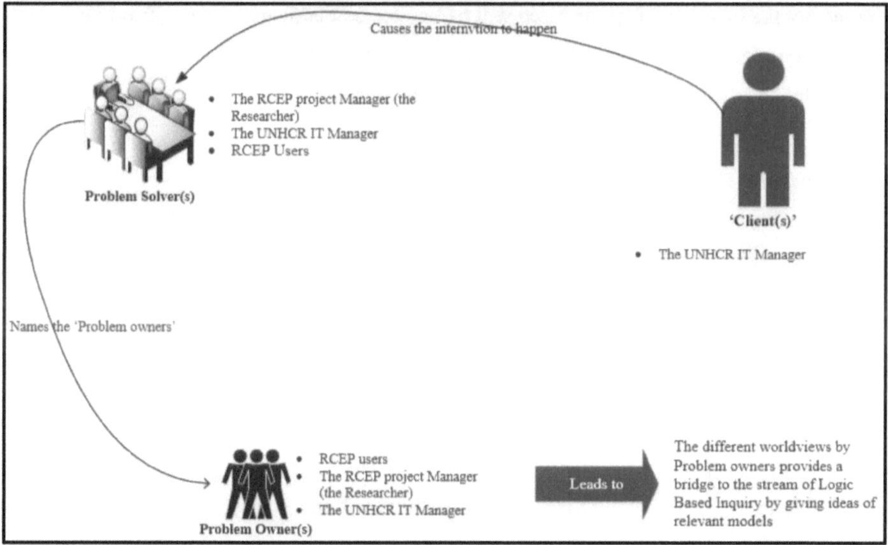

Figure 4.1: Analysis One: The RCEP Intervention itself

The 'Problem Solver':

The researcher by virtue of being the person participating in the inquiry process as both the researcher and participant in the form of RCEP project manager fits into the problem solver role. Equally, since the UNHCR IT Manager will be working closely with the researcher during the investigation, will also fall into the role 'problem solver'. The researcher and UNHCR project manager will need to involve the RCEP users in conducting the investigation and therefore the group will also fall into the problem solver role.

Problem Owner(s)

Through the interaction with the groups in the Problem solver role, the researcher managed to establish that the problem owners of the RCEP project were the RCEP users, the UNHCR IT manager and the Researcher. These are the same people occupying the role problem solvers. The users have a vested interest in the outcome of the project as they ultimately will be using the IT system. The system, from their perspective, should address their concerns, make their work easy and lastly improve productivity. The UNHCR IT manager viewed a system which the users will depend on in doing their work system which also solves the challenge of lack of collaboration by the users due to constant movement caused by the nature of their jobs. To the researcher the outcome of the research will be key for academic reasons but also in providing the direction the project should take. Thus, the three roles in Analysis 1 was filled and the next section looks at Analysis two of the cultural stream of analysis.

4.3.2 Analysis Two: RCEP Social Analysis

The second tool used in the cultural stream of analysis was Analysis two, the social analysis. This was conducted through formal interviews of RCEP users as stated in the methodology chapter and interview schedule shown in Appendix A. The three main elements that were inquired relevant to the RCEP project were

- General Questions: Related to the history, contingency, and formalisms within and of UNHCR.
- Role: Of Staff member in UNHCR.
- Norm: Expected staff behavior within UNHCR.
- Value: What constitutes good or bad behavior in UNHCR?

The researcher managed to have interviews with 14 RCEP users instead of the planned twenty-one. Those who could not give the interviews, three, were away on official work trips while two were on leave and the other refused citing possibility of being victimized by management. The formal interviews were conducted during working hours and the researcher would request the user approximately 30 minutes of their time. Most users would not accept to have their personal time used for these interviews and that is why there were conducted during working hours. Those staff members who had private offices, the interview was conducted in their offices however for those that shared offices, it was conducted in the researcher's office to ensure privacy. All the interviewees requested that their names remain anonymous and that whatever they said should never be recorded and seen by their supervisors. The same had been stressed before the interview, by the interviewer that all direct quotes will not be attributable to an individual, but that confidentiality will be maintained. There was a lot of fear within the users of victimization by the supervisors. Most of them indicated that because of the type of employment contract they had, there were afraid that if they say anything negative and it gets into the ears of senior management, their contracts might not be renewed. The interviewer assured the interviewee of their rights to attend or refuse the interview and that their names would never be used. This is how the interviews were conducted and some of the challenges that the interviewer faced. The next section outlines the findings of the interviews.

4.3.2.1 Social analysis ethnography interview findings: General Questions

History: Most interviewees cited the 1951 Refugee convention which gave birth to UNHCR as the most important date for the organization and one mentioned that "it is a question often asked in job interviews and perhaps one which all UNHCR employees should know". The repatriation of Mozambique refugees in the 1980s from South Africa back to their country is one past even which is fondly remembered by those who were present as very important. The 2008 Xenophobic attacks, in particular, are also cited as prominent for the organization by those participants who were present. One interviewee mentioned that, the Xenophobic attack of 2008 and subsequent ones put the organization on the spotlight and brought out the best out of most staff members who felt obliged to go out in the affected areas to assist. The value of togetherness was cited as a lesson learned from this episode and one which is now part of the organization. The questions around the reputation of IT department and previous projects that had been implemented brought a very negative picture in general. Most interviewees expressed lack of trust with the department. The migration from the Novell email system to Microsoft outlook system was a typical example that was used and one interviewee was very candid with the assessment, "the people in the IT department are not competent enough, can you believe that I lost more than 10 years of files and emails and nobody did anything about it". The feeling was also that the new systems are always complicated and never meant to improve how they work. SSM was never used in the past implementations and nobody knew if any particular methodology was used since everything was done haphazardly.

Contingency: Most users acknowledged that the bulk of the funding goes to the Protection department which forms the core function of the organization. As a result of the dependency of the organization on IT systems, most interviewees acknowledged that IT projects are given priority. However, some interviewees expressed sentiments that not all IT projects are critical and that some of them do not add any value to the organization. "They just make changes for the sake of it, tell me was there anything wrong with changing from GroupWise to Outlook"? This was in reference to moving from one email system to the other. Regarding the question on whether the RCEP project should be prioritized some interviewees felt there was no emergency to adopt it since the current system was not bad. Others felt that the idea to be able to collaborate was very good, however, the systems seemed to infringe on their rights and therefore should not be prioritized until the operating procedure was clear and agreed upon. The Country Director (Country Representative) had the ultimate say on which projects to undertake. This was the general sentiments from the interviewees regarding the question on who decides which projects to undertake. In relation to the current change procedure, most interviewees indicated that they did not know if there was a formal change procedure in place. What the only see are email explaining a new project to be implemented but do know if there is any laid down procedure on how to do it. Most interviewees expressed the need to be consulted before the project is implemented and also that they need explanation on how each project will be beneficial to the jobs.

Formalisms: Pertaining to the first question on which UNHCR policies were indispensable, most of the interviewees mentioned that the policies around the core values of the UN were not dispensable. The policy to respect diversity of the workplace was cited as one which the organization takes very seriously. In terms of structures within the organization which are important the interviewees mentioned that the distinction between one working as a local staff member and or an expatriate was historically recognized as important. Projects are generally selected based on the availability of funding, first and foremost. And, there are no clear laid down procedure on how change projects should be conducted. These were the sentiments from the interviews regarding selection and implementation of change projects. Most interviewees expressed ignorance on how IT projects should be implemented technically but insisted that they wish to be consulted, engaged first before any project is implemented and throughout the project. They were against having a project imposed on them without dialog. "If don't feel part of the project, why should support it, 1 will resist it, simple!" said one interviewee quite strongly.

4.3.2.2 Roles

Some of the interviewees were not very comfortable in sharing their roles fearing that it can later be linked to the findings of the research. Again, the researcher assured them of the confidentiality of the process and that there would not be reference to names of individuals. Some of the roles that the interviewees cited were:

- Programme Unit implementation roles
- Refugee Protection related roles; Child protection, Sexual, gender-based violence
- Refugee resettlement related roles
- Refugee registration roles
- Media and Public relations related roles
- Finance and HR related roles

Most of the interviewees had more than five years' experience with UNHCR while three had less than five years of UNHCR experience. In terms of combined UNHCR and non-UNHCR experience, most of the interviewees had more than five years of experience. By nature of the formal roles most of them were running projects in their departments especially those from the Protection and Programme departments. Communication was cited as key in implementing projects. This was cited by the interviewees who run projects daily. One interviewee mentioned that, "For UNHCR led projects with refugees to be a success, you have to ensure the refugees have a buy-in into the project. You have to have a shared view otherwise it will be doomed from the word go".

Regarding the questions around the actual roles that the interviewees will be holding most of them expressed that since it is a highly technical project their role is very limited. They, however, mentioned that they as long as their concerns are taken into consideration, participate in deciding what is good for them in the project and are part of the entire process through consultation they will support the project. Effective training was also mentioned as important in enabling ease of use of the system. The majority were not familiar with SSM and had not heard it before.

4.3.2.3 Norms

Most of the interviewees mentioned that the behaviour expected from a UNHCR staff member was the one that respect the diversity of the workplace. That UN staff members come from different cultures, backgrounds, beliefs, races etc. was important that the staff members respect that. The UN-wide values and competencies were cited as the ones that determines expected behaviour of all UN staff members including UNHCR. And, there were serious repercussions including dismissal if these rules were not followed. Most of the interviewees then indicated that, it will be the same values expected for anyone playing a role in the RCEP project. There were no key roles models that were mentioned, the interviewees found this question to be vague.

4.3.2.4 Values

This section looked at the questions around the values expected for UNHCR staff member and in particular for a RCEP role. Good behavior is regarded when one respects fellow staff in their diversity. Bad behavior is when staff has no respect for difference in diversity; religious beliefs, race, sexual orientation etc. Good behavior regarding new IT projects is when one shows willingness to learn new technology - a competency referred to as 'Continuous learning' in UNHCR parlance. Conformity to UNHCR's diverse staff members. Any objection to this risks contract non-renewal and therefore rebellion is very limited. Willingness to learn new technology will be regarded as positive engagement.

4.3.3 Analysis Three: RCEP Political Analysis

This section looks at the 'disposition of power, the nature of power and process by which power is obtained, exercised, preserved & passed on. The researcher tried to carry out the analysis using formal interviews, but the interviewees were not comfortable with the line of questions and after trying two interviews it was then decided to use informal interviewees. These were done partly as observations during meetings, lunches and informal gatherings. Informal interviews were also done during the same gatherings or when the researcher is invited to the interviewees' workstation for technical assistance. The next section summarizes the findings of the informal interviews.

4.3.3.1 Disposition of Power

Regarding the question on which department holds more power historically and currently, most interviewees were unanimous that the Protection department holds more power now and historically based on it being the core function of the organization. The IT department was viewed as wielding some considerable power by most participants mainly because most of the work activities requires IT involvement and also as custodians of the organizational confidential information. The UNHCR director was seen as the most powerful person in the organization currently and historically by virtue of being the most senior position in the country. Most of the interviewees agreed that power in the organization was obtained by the position that one occupies. The more senior the position the more powerful the person is. Equally, it was pointed out that those who work directly as subordinates of these people are equally powerful. One interviewee declared that, "the second most powerful person in the office has to be the director's executive assistant, if you need to know any important information go to her". The executive assistant therefore in this case would get the power informally. Most of the interviewees mentioned that the director still holds ultimate power to change and influence new projects, but one name kept cropping up of a person who held informal power to influence decision making. This person obtained her power from being close to the senior management and having the ability to speak her mind. It was observed that there were many cliques in the organization based on which country or region you come from, which religion you belong to, which department you belong, social life etc. For example, French speakers had their own clique, smokers had their on clique and would, during intervals, go to the smoking area together for a smoke break. It was also observed that some degree of power was obtained by belong to one of these cliques.

4.3.3.2 Nature of Power

The director, deputy director and Departmental heads have power to distribute resources. The head of the Finance department has some influence on which change projects to undertake.
It used to be the previous Project controller but ever since she left no one has the power to convince others on the need for new projects.

4.3.3.3 Process by which power is obtained, exercised, preserved & passed on

Most interviewees mentioned that the ultimate person with the power to distribute resources is the director and whoever has been delegated that power. One of the interviewees mentioned that if you want to get anything done you have to mention that you have been send by the director and most people will jump. Regarding the question around how power is obtained the consensus was that power within the organization was obtained by authority and association to those who wield the power. And this is also true when one belongs to a particular clique. Regarding the question on how power is exercised, it was the general sentiment that even though the organization tries to share information as much as possible, those who withheld information before it is disseminated exercised some power. It was the observation of the researcher that power was exercised through formal roles in the organization to a lesser extent to the clique you belong to because you will have access to certain information that others do not have. The questions on how power was preserved, got responses that the through formal roles where certain information was not shared to all the staff members, in such situations the senior management preserved power. Most interviewees agreed that there was no culture of politicking in the organization. In the question on how power was passed on, the consensus was that through formal means and delegation was power passed on. Power was also passed on informally through belonging to certain cliques where informal discussions took place. The next section looks at Analysis 1, 2 & 3 and attempts to illustrate it into a Rich Picture.

4.3.4 RCEP Rich Picture

Analysis 1, 2 & 3 as part of the cultural stream of analysis is hereby, in this section, illustrated by a Rich Picture to depict the problematical situation and is illustrated in Figure 4.2. At the very core the UNHCR IT manager feels that the RCEP users are not supportive of the project and would want to resist the project rendering it a failure. The RCEP Project Manager who is also the Researcher identifies the issue as not clearly defined and therefore offers to use SSM to improve the problematical situation. On the RCEP users' perspective they feel that the project violates their rights and should be resisted. If they had been consulted from the beginning and might have felt part of the project. The UNHCR Director is identified as the most powerful position in the organization which decides which projects to receive funding. Traditionally the Protection department is the preferred department and receives the bulk of the funding from the organization. The core values of the UN, with the Diversity, at the center, is identified as the most important value in the organization that should be respected. In terms of History of the organization the 1951 UN convention that gave birth to the United Nations High Commissioner for Refugees (UNHCR) as a UN agency is sighted as the most historical moment in the organization. Hence the Refugee protection is the core business of UNHCR. The RCEP users feel that they were never consulted on the RCEP project and therefore the negative attitude about the project. The IT department from the RCEP users' perspective should never be trusted based on the history of past projects which did not go so well. They feel that their needs are never considered but in fact projects are each time imposed on them.

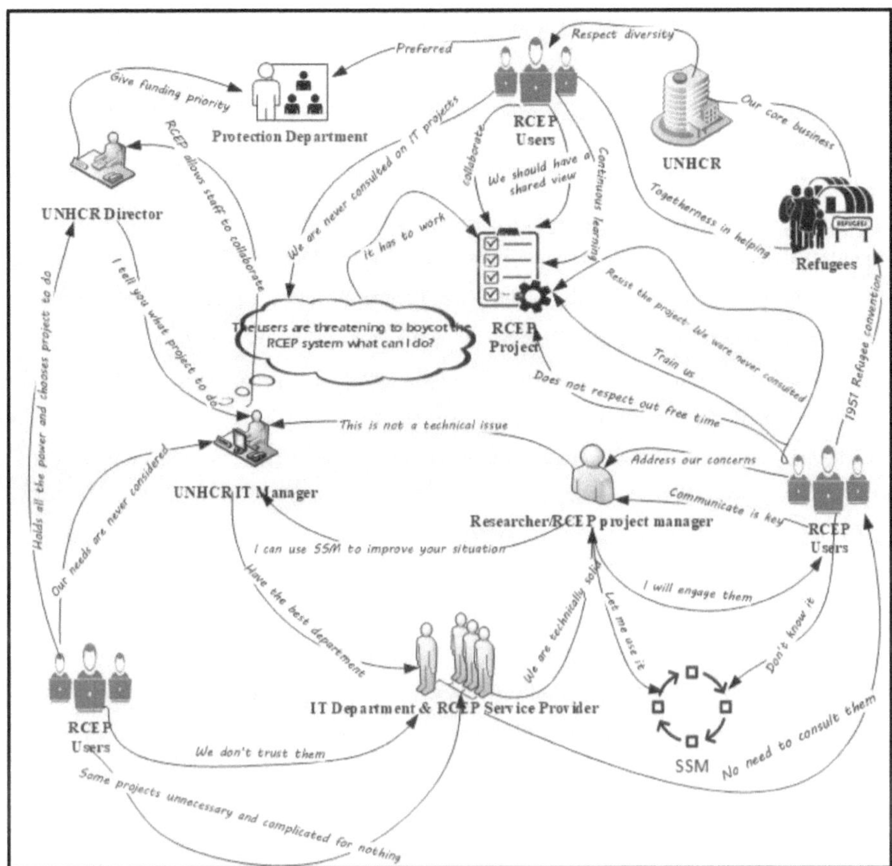

Figure 4.2: RCEP Rich Picture

On the part of the IT department and the service provider assisting with the RCEP project, they feel they are technically proficient and do not see the need to consult with the RCEP users. A sentiment shared by the project manager. On other hand the Project manager feels that if Change management skills of communication through consulting, dialoging and engaging the users is employed the problematic situation can be improved. Equally some of the RCEP users who are deal with projects in their departments acknowledge that communication in any project is key to success.

4.3.5 Conclusion of the stream of cultural enquiry

The stream of cultural enquiry analysis is not, "done once and then stored for reference in a systems study. It is essential that they are continually updated and developed as the intervention progresses" (Jackson, 2003: 190). The analysis was captured in the form of a rich picture, which in itself is also continuously updated. The Problem owners' Worldviews identified above and illustrated in the Rich Picture provides the bridge to the logic stream of analysis the focus of the next section.

4.4 THE STREAM OF LOGIC-BASED ENQUIRY

The stream of cultural analysis' 1, 2 and 3 above was captured into the rich picture to pictorially present the problematical situation. The Rich Picture provides insights on what relevant systems can be derived. This section looks at the relevant systems based on the worldviews of the problem owners and come up with the Logic stream of analysis. The analysis will be conducted through a one-day workshop that will bring together the RCEP users, the UNHCR IT Manager and the RCEP Project manager who is also the researcher and workshop facilitator.

4.4.1 Planning for RCEP one-day Workshop

The Researcher and the UNHCR IT Manager sat down to discuss how the one-day workshop was to be conducted. An email inviting all the RCEP users was sent explaining the purpose and benefits of the workshop but emphasizing that it was voluntary and for academic and departmental purposes. Most importantly explaining the confidentiality of the deliberations and its outcome. It was agreed that the workshop will start at 0900hrs and finish at 1630hrs in the UNHCR Pretoria office main boardroom. Normal working hours for the staff is from 0800hrs until 1700hrs. Since attendance of the workshop was voluntary, the agreed workshop schedule gave the staff members some time to attend to their daily responsibilities. It was decided that the UNHCR IT Manager would open the workshop and he wanted to emphasize the need for the participants to own the process and also to freely to speak up. The Researcher/RCEP Project Manager would lead the proceedings in a facilitator and participant role. A projector and flip charts were made available for the workshop and participants were told not to bring anything to the workshop since the process will follow, to a large extent, the logic reasoning on the part of participants. The following procedure was agreed on how the workshop would be conducted. Naming of the relevant system will be done first, whether it's a 'primary task' or 'issue-based'. Formulation of the 'Root Definition using CATWOE and PQR formula techniques will follow based on the cultural stream of analysis. Then a conceptual model will be constructed while a monitoring and control system using the 3E's will be used. Finally, comparison between the model and reality will be done, notionally, by operating the model and performing the activities.

4.4.2 RCEP SSM One-Day Workshop

The workshop started at about 0915hrs with twelve participants in attendance. Out of the total 21 possible attendants only 12 showed up and it was agreed that it was good a number to have the workshop. Flip charts, whiteboard and projector screen were made available for use. The UNHCR IT Manager made the opening remarks thanking all the participants for their participation. He reiterated the importance of confidentiality and anonymity during the entire process and that the participants should speak and not fear victimization. It was also mentioned that the researcher who was also played the role of facilitator and project manager was only there to facilitate but not to prescribe the process to be taken. The researcher was then given the floor and reaffirmed the same ethical considerations made by the UNHCR IT Manager. It was explained that while an SSM enquiry will be followed the participants do not need to fully understand how SSM works but the facilitator will guide the process. The first one and half hours of the morning was to be taken recapping the findings of the cultural stream of analysis which will lead into the creation of the Root Definition. The afternoon was set aside for the creation of the conceptual model and the comparison of the model and perceived reality.

4.4.2.1 Discussion of the findings of the Cultural stream of analysis

The Researcher started by presenting his findings from the cultural analysis and opened the discussion. The rich picture drew a lot of discussion with the participants feeling that the lack of consultation and involvement of the project on the users was a serious concern for them. It was then agreed that the findings reflected the sentiments of most of the participants. The RCEP project cuts across all the UNHCR functional departments and therefore is issue-based. The next stage was to derive the Root Definition (RD) based on the issues raised in the cultural stream of analysis. The next section illustrates how the RD was created using the PQR formula and enriching it with the Mnemonic CATWOE.

4.4.2.2 'PQR Formula'

The researcher explained that to help come up with a prose to describe the relevant system to be modelled, the PQR formula was to be used. Where the formula was to help identify what was to be done, the transformation process and why it was to be done. To kick start the discussion, the facilitator suggested a Root Definition that was to be used as a starting point. The Root Definition is as follows:

A RCEP users-owned system to change the way the RCEP project is being implemented by ensuring the project manager consults and engages the users throughout the project in order for the users to have a shared view of the project.

The facilitator explained that the worldview espoused in the Root Definition was from the from the RCEP users' perspective who were one of the problem owners identified in the cultural stream of analysis. The 'What' captured in the do P was to change the way the RCEP project was currently being implemented. The transformation process, which is the Q in the 'How', was ensuring the RCEP project manager consulted and engaged the users throughout the project. The reason for the transformation as captured by Q was in order for the users to have a shared view on what the project entailed and thereby avoid user resistance and, in the process, avoid project failure. The suggested Root Definition generated a lot of debate and the participants suggested changes that were to be made. The participants felt that the P in the suggested Root Definition did not fully capture their perspective as it just suggested change of the way the RCEP was being implemented in general terms. The also felt the transformation process did fully capture what they feel the project manager should do to ensure that the RCEP users are fully onboard. The workshop Root Definition is and the logic behind is explained in the next section.

4.4.2.3 Naming Relevant Systems: The RCEP Root Definition and CATWOE

Pursuant to the debate that ensued the participants settled on the Root Definition as given in this section, the PQR outcome was updated. The logic behind was that the Worldview (W) was that of the RCEP users who felt that consultation, dialog and their participation would lead to a shared view of how the RCEP project will be implemented. The 'P' was the addressing of the concerns the RCEP users had with the current modality of implementing the RCEP project. How this was to be done, which is the 'Q' was through making sure the project manager fully communicates with the users throughout the life of the project. And finally, the 'R' was in order to ensure the users had part ownership to the project. The RCEP Root Definition is as follows:

A RCEP users-owned system to address the concerns of RCEP users by ensuring the RCEP project manager consults, dialog, engages and allows user participation throughout the project's life in order for the users to have a shared view of the project and avoid failure.

To further enrich the Root Definition the Mnemonic CATWOE was used. At the very core of the CATWOE Mnemonic is the Transformation (T) and Worldview (W). In the RD the Transformation was the need to address the RCEP users' concerns with the current RCEP project transformed to the RCEP users' concerns addressed. The Worldview espoused in the Transformation process was that of the RCEP users who believed that this transformation will ensure they have a buy-in giving the part ownership to the entire process instead of it being imposed on them. The rest of the analysis is as follows.

- 'C': The beneficiaries of the RCEP project are the RCEP users
- 'A': The actors are the Project Manager and his team who will implement the RCEP project.
- 'T': The need to address the RCEP users' concerns → Need met by ensuring the RCEP project manager fully communicates and involves the RCEP users in the entire process.
- 'W': The declared worldview relevant to the RCEP project is the RCEP users believe that the needs are addressed they will have a shared view of the project thereby ensuring that they have a buy-in into the project thereby avoiding user resistance.
- 'O': The owners of the RCEP project is the UNHCR Project Manager, the RCEP users and the RCEP Project Manager.
- 'E': The environmental constraints include the availability of funding for the project, the time required to complete the project.

The 3Es: The 3Es relevant to the RCEP project are:

- **Efficacy**: There is less resistance to the RCEP project by the users. The users feel there is shared ownership to the entire process, a shared view of the project.
- **Efficiency**: Judgement by UNHCR IT Manager that the RCEP project was implemented using minimum resources considering the outcome.
- **Effectiveness**: Judgement by UNHCR IT Manager that the long-term goal of the RCEP project is being met and that the RCEP user found the system useful and are using it.

Now that the workshop had come up with an agreed Root Definition the afternoon session, after lunch, was dedicated to the coming up with the RCEP conceptual model. The RD was used as the basis for the RCEP Conceptual model and the next section looks at the model in greater detail.

4.4.3.4 Modelling Relevant System: The RCEP Conceptual Model

The facilitator guided the participants to use logic only based on the Root Definition developed and without any relation to the real world. The workshop first looked at three broad activities; the current state of the project, the transformation to be made and the desired state of the project. These activities were all derived from the Root Definition. Figure 4.3 shows the RCEP Conceptual model, the output from the workshop.

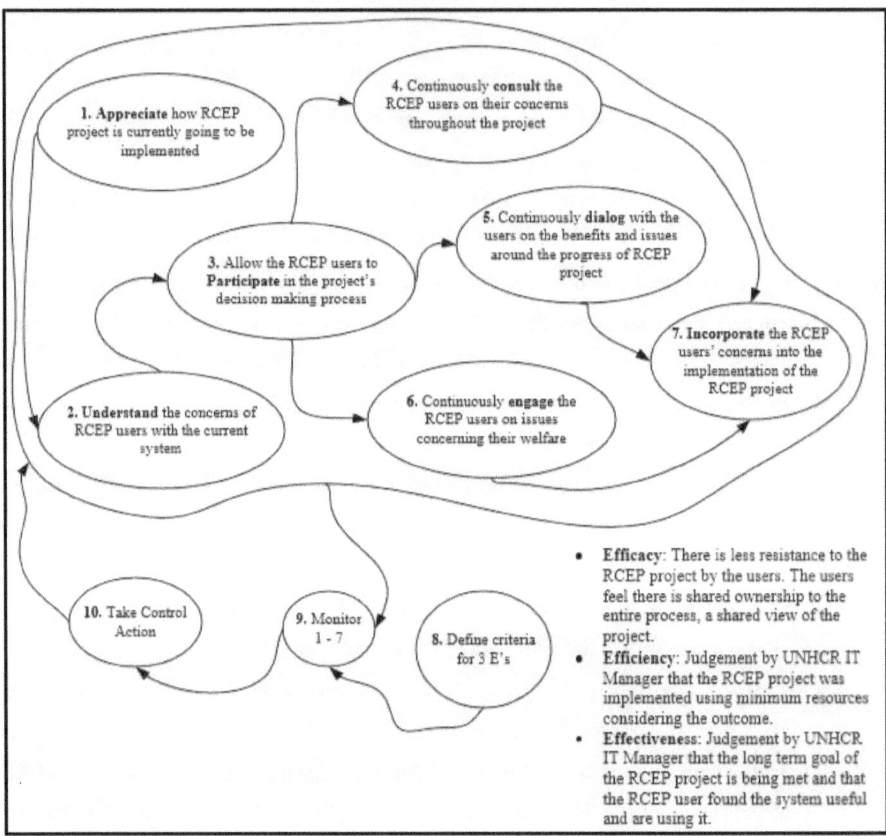

Figure 4.3: The RCEP Conceptual Model

The verbs to indicate the action required in each activity are in bold. The activities around the current state as depicted in the Root Definition are activity 1 & 2. Activities 3, 4, 5 & 6 are the activities to perform the transformation while the desired state is depicted by activity 7. The activities in the current state looks to a large extent the need to have a good appreciation of the current state. The transformation activities, on the other hand equips the project manager with soft skills to a large extent involve the users in the running of the project. The desired state is when the concerns of the RCEP users are incorporated into the project and thereby the users having a shared view of the project.

In terms of monitoring and controlling the activities in the model, the need to see if the means depicted in the model works, the Efficacy. This is shown by users' less resistance to the system and the users feeling a sense of ownership to the problem. The efficient use of the resources relative to the outcome in as far as knowing the resources were used efficiently. The long-term goal, as depicted by the Effectiveness of the model is shown by the actual use of the system in the long run. It is the judgement of the UNHCR IT Manager in the end, on all the 3Es that will be critical to see if the monitoring and control is working and ultimately according to the model.

To ensure that the RCEP conceptual model was 'defensible' every activity in the model was checked to see if it can be linked back to the Root Definition and vice-versa every phrase in the RD was also checked to see if it led to an activity in the model. Necessary changes were made during the cross examination to ensure that the model was sorely derived from the RD and the CATWOE. After satisfactorily concluding that the RCEP conceptual model was defensible the notional comparison with reality was conducted and this is covered in the next section.

4.4.4.3 Comparing the RCEP Conceptual Model with Perceived Reality
Due to time constraints in the afternoon of the workshop it was decided by the researcher to change the plan from notionally modeling the activities but instead to adopt the comparison matrix. Table 4.1 shows the RCEP Conceptual model comparison matrix which attempts to compare the activities in the model with the perceived reality. The facilitator listed all the activities in the left most column and these were to be compared with the perceived reality in terms of whether the activity existed in real life or not, if it does how the activity is being done and the measures of performance. Based on that the participants would come up with a set of recommendations for each activity and any comments would be included in the comments column.

Activity 1 was perceived to partly exist but specifically from a technical point of view. The project manager and the project team had a very good appreciation of the RCEP project technically but not from a social perspective. The recommendation was to ensure that the project team had a holistic appreciation of what the RCEP project entails. Activity 2 relates to the understanding of the concerns raised by the RCEP users regarding the RCEP project and specifically how it affected them as illustrated in the stream of cultural analysis. The activity was also found to partly exist in the perceived reality. The fact that the UNHCR IT manager had sensed that there was a simmering resistance to the project and hence the need to conduct the research showed that there was, in part, an attempt to understand the concerns of the RCEP users. Formal and informal interviews with the RCEP users to capture their feedback on the project were recommendation s that were pointed to try and have a more formal way to fully understand RCEP users' concerns. The participation of RCEP users in the project, Activity 3, was found to be nonexistent in the perceived reality. It was however the recommendation that the RCEP users as both the project owners and beneficiaries should participate in the project formally throughout the life of the project if they are going to have any buy-in into the project. It was noted in the comments that this takes a total mentality change from the project manager to see the users as participants and not only as recipients and user s of the system.

Table 4.1: RCEP Conceptual model comparison matrix

Activities from the RCEP Conceptual model	Exist in perceived reality?	How the activity is done	Measures of performance	Recommendations	Comments
Activity 1 – *Appreciate how the RCEP project is currently going to be implemented*	Partly	Activity is being done only from the technical perspective. The Project manager and his team do have a solid appreciation of the project but not from the users' social perspective	Check to see if there is a holistic appreciation of how the RCEP project will be implemented.	Over and above the technical perspective of the project the project manager should equally have an appreciation of the social side.	The appreciation of the RCEP project is not only the technical side but also the people side in terms of the beneficiaries of the project, the RCEP users.
Activity 2 – *Understand the concerns of the RCEP users with the current implementation plan.*	Partly	The UNHCR IT Manager has some understanding of the concerns that the RCEP users have hence the research study however the gathering of this information was not done in a structured manner.	Check to see that the RCEP users' concerns have been captured in full.	Conduct formal and informal interviews with RCEP users to have a good understanding of the concerns that they have with the project.	This is at the core of the cultural stream of analysis to capture what the users' concerns are. While technical feedback is important the social feedback from the beneficiaries is important.
Activity 3 – *Allow the RCEP users to Participate in the project's decision-making process.*	No	None	None	Ensure the users as the main beneficiaries of the project participate in the project from project proposal to project closure	Change of mentality is required from a top-down approach to an inclusive one.

Activity					
Activity 4 – *Continuously consult the RCEP users on their concerns throughout the project*	Partly	The UNHCR IT Manager got to hear about the possible resistance of the project by the users through rumour.	None	Continuously consult with the RCEP users through formal and informal means to understand their concerns	None
Activity 5 – Continuously dialog with the users on the benefits and issues around the progress of the RCEP project	No	None	None	Do formal and informal dialog with the users explaining the benefits of the project and the issues the project faces	None
Activity 6 – Continuously engage the RCEP users on issues concerning their welfare	No	None	None	Engage the users formally and informally to ensure they feel part of the process	Engagement is continuous
Activity 7 – Incorporate the RCEP users; concerns into the implementation of the RCEP project	No	None	None	Ensure user resistance to the RCEP project has been significantly reduced to avoid project failure	This is a continuous process

Activity 4 which relates to the need to continuously consult the RCEP users throughout the life of the project was found to partly exist in the perceived reality. The informal consultation by the UNHCR IT Manager to find out about the project which led to the research was seen to represent some form of consultation albeit very minimum. It was the recommendation that the both formal and informal consultations with the users should be done continuously. Activity 5, and 6 were found to be totally non-existent in the project hence meaning there was not dialog, engagement from the part of the project manager with the RCEP users. It was recommended that formal dialog through meetings and interviews was essential to show that the concerns of the users were taken seriously. Consequently, Activity 7, which relates to the consolidation of the feedback from the users into a RCEP project implementation plan that aims to meet and address the users' concerns was not existent. It was therefore the recommendation these concerns are addressed, avoided and minimized.

The comparison brought an end to the one-day SSM workshop and the facilitator thanked the participants for their corporation and handed over the platform to the UNHCR IT Manager. He reiterated the confidentiality of the outcome and explained that the recommendations given will be compiled by the researcher to actions to address the users' concerns and improve the situation. The workshop was thus closed with the message that the interaction should be continuous to ensure their concerns are addressed.

4.5 CONCLUSION

The chapter followed the two streams of SSM enquiry; the stream of cultural analysis and the logic-based stream of analysis as set out in the methodology chapter. Analysis 1, 2 & 3 fed into the Rich Picture which pictorially represented the problematic situation. The Worldview view expressed by the RCEP users, one of the 'problem owners' gave insight into the relevant system which was used to create the Root Definition as part of the one-day SSM workshop to tackle the logic-based stream of analysis. The resultant structured discussion which arose when comparing the activities in the conceptual model created and the perceived reality gave rise to a set of recommendations on improving the problematical situation. It is the basis of the next chapter to then identify the nature of improvements to the problematical situation which are both culturally feasible and systematically desirable. If the improvements are not accommodated by the users, then the SSM inquiry will start again.

CHAPTER 5: CONCLUSIONS AND RECOMMENDATIONS

5.1 INTRODUCTION

As a recap to the preceding chapters. The context within which this study is conducted is against a backdrop of poor performances by IT projects, in general, where two in three projects fail (Standish Group, 2016). The IT Manager for United Nations High Commissioner for Refugees (UNHCR), at its regional office for Southern Africa, is in the process of introducing a new IT collaboration system called RCEP but unfortunately the intended users of the system threaten to resist the system and thereby rendering it a failure. The IT manager does not doubt the technical capability of the project team in delivering the system but recognizes that he might be presented with a wider problem. The RCEP project manager, this researcher, posits that the problematical situation faced by the department is not clearly defined but is a human situation that can possibly be improved by integrating project management and change management. The researcher proposes to investigate the possibility of equipping the Project manager with the Change Management skill of communication to try and in improve the problematical situation. It is, therefore, the purpose of the study to perform this investigation to try and improve the situation.

The study attempts to answer four research questions to the study around how the problematical situation can be improved. The first question looks at how the project manager can be equipped with the change management skill of communication. The second and third question then looks at the different perspectives of the RCEP users to the problematical situation and what action can be done to improve the situation. Finally, the last question looks at other themes and perspectives that can emerge from the study.

The review of literature around the issue of user resistance and IT projects failure does establish that there is a wider emphasis by IT project managers on the technical hard side of IT projects and neglecting the social side of the projects as represented by Change management (Kerzner and Kerzner, 2017). SSM is identified as a methodology that deals with fuzzy and unstructured problematical situations (Checkland and Scholes, 1999; Checkland and Poulter, 2006). The problematical situation faced by the UNHCR IT manager falls into the description of unstructured, non-linear problematical situations that SSM deals with. Thus, an SSM investigation was identified as most appropriate.

The next section looks at the findings of the study and attempts to find a link with the literature review findings to draw conclusions.

5.2 RESEARCH CONCLUSIONS

This section attempts to draw conclusions from the research findings and how these are linked to the research questions and literature review. The intended result is to see if the research objectives have been met.

5.2.1 Research Question 1

The first research question is restated here as, *"How to equip project managers with the change management skill of communication to avoid IT project failure?"* This question attempts to investigate the modalities of equipping a project manager with change management skill of communication. Based on the background to the study, the question assumes that project managers and in this case, IT project managers, do not possess adequate training in change management (Cicmil, 1999; Hornstein, 2015). It is therefore the intention of the study to try and find out how best to equip the project manager with such a skill. Alternatively, this can be looked from the perspective of what competencies should the project manager demonstrate when they possess the skill of communication from change management. The lack of consensus in literature in how the two disciplines of project management and change management can work together is in agreement with this research question (Crawford and Nahmias, 2010; Jarocki, 2011; Pollack and Algeo, 2015). While in literature there is ground to believe that this integration can lead to reduction in the rate of project failure what is in question is how, practically, this can be done. Therefore, based on the above, the objective of the research related to this question is restated here; *"To explore an appropriate methodology to equip project managers with the change management skill of Communication"*.

5.2.1.1 Research Question Finding

The research used SSM, using Action Research, to equip the project manager with the change management skill of Communication. The researcher had a dual role of participant and researcher. To meet the truth criterion a research framework was clearly defined and followed through the SMM cultural and logic stream of analysis to ensure that the process is 'recoverable'. The cultural and logic stream of analysis, in the SSM investigation centered primarily on how and if it is important for the project manager to be equipped with the change management skill of communication. The interview questions in the cultural stream of analysis particularly probed to find out if the communication skill was relevant. The relevant system that gave insight into the root definition and subsequently the RCEP conceptual model clearly articulated what was required of the project manager. It is the finding of the study that the project manager, if the RCEP project was to avoid failure, was supposed to ensure the RCEP users participate in the decision making of the project, are consulted on the issues pertaining to the project that affects them, are consulted throughout the project and finally that the project manager engages and dialog with the users throughout the life of the project. Therefore, SSM is found to be the appropriate methodology to equip the project manager with the change management skill of Communication based on the study meeting the 'truth criterion'.

5.2.1.2 Discussion

The problematical situation facing the UNHCR IT manager is not well defined and fuzzy, but there is a clear feeling that something needs to be done to improve the situation hence the research. This is in agreement with Checkland and Scholes (1990) who found that human problem situations as a result of different perspectives to the situation often requires an improvement that accommodates the different opinions rather than a solution. Furthermore, the 'Truth Criterion" of 'recoverability' as opposed to 'repeatability' found in physical sciences, is met in this study based on the clearly defined research framework (Checkland and Scholes, 1990; Peter and Sue, 1998; Checkland and Poulter, 2006). This indeed shows the appropriateness of the methodology to this study.

It, therefore, can be concluded from the research finding that to equip the project manager with the change management skill of communication the project manager should consult, engage, dialog and ensure participation of the RCEP users if the project was to avoid failure. The social skills that the project manager should possess is in agreement the findings of Lehmann (2010) who defined communication in the change management field as the ability to debate, dialog, consult and engage. Gill (2002), is also in agreement but uses slight different words but with the same meaning that the project manager should empower users and convince them and finally share a vision. Kotter (1995), by the same token, sees the communication being demonstrated by the creation and subsequent communication of a vision followed by empowering others to act upon that vision through creating enabling structures for change. Therefore, it is incumbent upon the project manager to create such an enabling environment that allows the users to fully participate in the project. The communication of the vision of the project, which is done through consultation, engaging and debating with the end users empowers the users to feel part of the decision-making process and ultimately the owners of the project. This is opposed to the current environment that the participants of the SSM workshop and interviews during the cultural stream of analysis where the users feel the project being imposed on them. The users during the interview did acknowledge that IT projects are highly technical, and they do not understand that side of the project but still they need to be consulted and engaged. This is a clear sign that the vision of the project was not clearly articulated and communicated to the users. The enabling environment that the project manager should create is in agreement to the participative technique which is regarded as the most effective method of handling user resistance through the use of two way communication, information sharing, and consultation (Waddell and Sohal, 1998; Ali et al., 2016). This in essence defines and demonstrates communication as seen from the lenses of change management where the project manager share their vision, empower users and convince them (Gill, 2002).

Therefore, it can be concluded that by ensuring that the project manager has the ability to articulate a vision and then create an enabling environment that empowers and allows the participation of the users in sharing of that vision, demonstrates that the project manager is fully equipped with the change management skill of communication. The findings of the study, in this regard do fully answer the research question and meets the objective to "*To explore an appropriate methodology to equip project managers with the change management skill of Communication*".

5.2.2 Research Question 2
The second question is restated here; "*What world views are expressed by the Users in regard to the social problem facing the UNHCR RCEP project?*" Human situations inherently exhibits different and often times conflicting perspectives to a problematical situation (Checkland and Scholes, 1990; Checkland and Holwell, 1998; Checkland and Scholes, 1999; Checkland and Poulter, 2006). Hence this study being a human situation, the RCEP users inherently have different perspectives. Therefore this research question, as espoused by Checkland and Scholes (1999), intends to look at these 'Weltanschauung' or worldviews that the RCEP users have towards the introduction of the new RCEP software. The question further, apart from the worldviews, specifically defines the issue as a social problem. This is critical as this part of the question departs from a natural science perspective where problems are well defined and with defined objectives Yeo (1993); Crawford *et al.* (2003) and hence solutions. This part of the question,

therefore, takes cognizance of the unstructured, fuzzy and non-linear nature of a social situation which therefore sees the different and conflicting 'Weltanschauung' to the problematical situation as espoused by (Checkland, 1989; Crawford *et al.*, 2003). Therefore, the research question, attempts to identify the different and conflicting worldviews by the RCEP users to human social problematical situation. The research objective related to this question is therefore restated here, "*To identify the different world views expressed by the RCEP Users regarding the social problem facing the project*".

5.2.2.1 Research Question Finding

Analysis one, two and three, under the cultural stream of analysis, is synthesized in to the SSM rich picture in figure 4.2. It is the worldviews expressed by the RCEP users to the social problem which are depicted in the Rich picture and therefore attempts to answer this research question. These insights are then fed into the logic stream of analysis. It is the findings of the research in relation to this question, firstly, that the RCEP users feel that they are never consulted when a new IT system is being introduced and this is the case with the RCEP system. The users feel that the decision to introduce a new system is imposed on them without any consultation or their input. Examples were given of previous IT systems like the email system which was changed and yet the users felt the existing system was working well and meeting their needs. It is the findings of the research that the RCEP users feel that the new system infringes into their free time away from work. The feeling is that with the introduction of the new system the separation between official business hours and private free time will be blurred. It is also the finding of the research from the cultural stream of analysis around the question of trust and reputation of the IT department that the users felt that the department cannot be trusted and that some of the systems introduced are complicated and unnecessary. It is the overarching finding of the research that ties all the worldviews of the RCEP users that they feel that their views are never considered and that the RCEP project manager should address their concerns if there are to have a shared view of the project.

5.2.2.2 Discussion

The lack of consultation by the RCEP project team with the RCEP users is typical way of implementing IT projects. This is in agreement with Leeman (2014) who research finds out that the focus for most project managers is the technical side of the project and never on the social side. The emphasis is mostly on the technical design and implementation of the system. This ties in well with the key success factors around project management that of Time, Cost and performance, the triple constraint (Nicholas and Steyn, 2012; Project Management Institute, 2013) (Shenhar *et al.*, 2001; Cooke-Davies, 2002). As long as the triple constraint is met the project is deemed a success and equally as long as the system is deemed technical good then it can be imposed on the users. The lack of debate, dialog and a shared vision of the project leads to RCEP users feeling that the system is being imposed on them and that it infringes into the private free time away from the office. This is at the very core of the change management skill of communication that in order to have a shared vision of a project there needs to be the participation of the users in the decision process through a project (Lehmann, 2010). The lack of communication between the project manager and the RCEP users leads to the lack of trust between the two parties including the perception that the projects are unnecessary and complicated particularly as a result of past projects where the users were never consulted. The different perspectives or worldviews as expressed by the users is in agreement with Checkland and Scholes (1999) who sees problematic human situations such as the RCEP project as complex as a result of competing and conflicting perceptions about what constitutes the situation based on each person's assumptions, background, beliefs and other factors. It is also important to note that, as a result of these conflicting worldviews, human situations like the RCEP problematical situation do not yield a consensus or a solution but an improvement that accommodates these different interests (Checkland and Scholes, 1990).

The Worldviews as expressed by the users, in this study, to the social human situation facing the RCEP project, therefore, do meet the research objective to *"To identify the different world views expressed by the RCEP Users regarding the social problem facing the project"*.

5.2.3 Research Question 3

The third question is restated here, *"What action can be taken to improve the problem situation?"* Now that the study has looked, in question 2 above, the different worldviews by the users in relation to the RCEP social problem situation, this research question in turn, intends to investigate the actions that can be taken by the project manager to improve the situation. Research question 1 had looked at how the project manager can be equipped with the change management skill of communication and now this question looks at the concrete steps that can actually be taken to improve the situation. This question is right at the core of the social problem situation that the UNHCR IT project manager is presented with that of possible failure due to possible user resistance. This is what the Checkland and Scholes (1990) refers as the action to improve the problematical situation. The objective of this research question in the study is "to discover what action can be taken to alleviate the initial social problem".

5.2.3.1 Research Question Finding

The RCEP Rich Picture synthesizes the cultural stream of analysis and Table 4.1, the RCEP conceptual model comparison matrix, brings together the research findings from the cultural stream of analysis and the logic stream of analysis. The comparison matrix looks at the gaps between the conceptual model from the RCEP SSM workshop and how the RCEP project is actually being implemented. The findings regarding this question is that the project manager needs to first have a full appreciation of how the project is being implemented from a social perspective and most importantly from the RCEP users' perspective. This is also linked with the second finding that RCEP project manager needs to have a full understanding of the concerns raised by the RCEP users regarding how the implementation of the RCEP project is being done. The project manager, therefore, in the two findings needs to conduct formal and informal interviews with the RCEP users to have a full understanding and appreciation of their project social side and the concerns of the users.

It is also the study's finding that the project manager does not consult, engage, dialog and debate with the RCEP users, the beneficiaries of the IT system. The perception of the users, as shown in the cultural stream of analysis, is that most often new systems are imposed on the users by the UNHCR IT department without consulting. Therefore, the actual action as espoused in the comparison between the conceptual model and the RCEP project is that the users need to be consulted, engaged, have dialog and have debate from project initiation until project closure. This means the interaction between the project manager and the users is a continuous process during the entire life of the project. Finally, it is the finding of the research as an actual action to be taken to improve the RCEP problem situation is to incorporate all these concerns raised by the users into the implementation of the RCEP project.

In the Rich Picture, training was also identified as an important action that can be taken to ensure the users are confident in using the system. When the interviewees were asked the roles they will be playing in the new RCEP project they mentioned how the system was highly technical and therefore they felt limited to find a specific role. There was also mention how some of the system that was introduced in the past was complicated and, in their view, unnecessary. Therefore, it was the finding that training will assist in ensuring the RCEP users are confident in the use of the system and also in perception about the system.

5.2.3.2 Discussion

The RCEP project manager is faced with a possible rebellion against the project as a result of lack of trust, perception that the project is being imposed and also the perception that IT projects are complicated and unnecessary. This is a typical example of user resistance which is an adverse reaction to the introduction of an IT system (Markus, 1983; Hirschheim and Newman, 1988; Kim and Kankanhalli, 2009). Kim and Kankanhalli (2009) reported that the organization IT toolbox conducted a survey of 375 organization and found out that user resistance was the number one ranked cause for IT failure in large IT projects such as enterprise resource planning (ERP) systems. Additionally, the current implementation strategy that the UNHCR IT manager and RCEP project manager are pursuing where the users feel that the project and previous project is imposed on them without consultation is in agreement with the Coercive approach by (Ali *et al.*, 2016) which looks to reduce user resistance through coercion. Therefore, the findings of the research agree that the RCEP project is facing possible user resistance. The subsequent, the actions proposed by the research to use in a bid to improve the RCEP problem situation is in agreement with the Participative approach to user resistance. Vision sharing, feedback, empowering of users and consultation are at the center of the empowering approach (Mumford and Weir, 1979; Chang *et al.*, 2013; Ali *et al.*, 2016). This also ties to the Interaction Failure category of IT project failure by Lyytinen and Hirschheim (1988) which takes cognizance of the people side of the project; the attitude of the users.

Klaus and Blanton (2010), identified training as critical in reducing the level of resistance from users. This can be as a result of lack of requisite skills to use the new system or negative perception (Besson and Rowe, 2001). Klaus and Blanton (2010) goes on further to say that the quality of the training and timing is also critical in ensuring the negative perception is not reinforced. Therefore, the findings of the study in relation to this research question do meet the research objective in coming up with actions that the project manager needs to take to improve the problem situation.

5.3 RECOMMENDATIONS

This section consolidates the research findings, the conclusions of the research based on the cultural stream of analysis and the logic stream of analysis and its relation to literature and come up with recommendations.

Recommendation 1- Training

The outcome of the cultural stream of analysis which is captured in the Rich picture emphasizes the need for training. The perception by the users that most new IT systems are unnecessary and complicated can be debunked by effective training. For the training to be effective timing is crucial (Klaus and Blanton, 2010). Due to the RCEP users perceiving the new system as highly technical, training, must be conducted prior to the launch of the new systems and thereafter continuously until the users are comfortable and confident in using the system. The training can also be contacted in targeted groups instead of in one big group considering that the staff have a fear to speak up.

Recommendation 2 – Understand the concerns of the RCEP users

Based on the findings of the research it is recommended that the RCEP project manager has a full understanding of the concerns that being raised by the RCEP users with the way the RCEP project is being implemented. These concerns can be identified through formal and informal interviews with the users. The existing way of discovering these concerns which is mainly based on rumor does not work, it needs a more structured way to establish the social issues around the problem situation.

Recommendation 3 – Participation in decision making process

Based on the findings of the research the users feel left out of the process. Most of the decision affecting them are imposed on them without their input. It is therefore advised that the project manager let the RCEP users participate in the decision-making process of the project regarding the issues that affect them. This will go a long way in reducing the negative feeling around the project and allow the users to claim part ownership to the project.

Recommendation 4 – Consult, dialog, debate

The main finding of the research is the need for the project manager to open up the project to the users to allow consultation, dialog, debate and engagement with the users. This defines communication as stipulated in the change management discipline. This interaction with the users allows vision sharing and ultimately buy-in from the users into the project and most importantly reduce the level of user resistance.

Recommendation 5 – Incorporate user's concern into project implementation

Finally, it is important, after taking into consideration the concerns raised by the RCEP users to actually do something about them. There is need to incorporate the actions to improve the situation above into how the project is implemented. While the incorporation of the actions above will bring about improvement in the problem situation it is important to note that it will not bring about consensus among the users since divergent worldviews will still exist but it will bring them closer to an improved problem situation, an accommodation which they can all live with.

5.4 FURTHER AREAS OF STUDY

A number of studies identified the integration of project management and change management as a possible panacea to the dismal performance of IT projects. This research as a result of time only focused on change management skill of communication. There are other competencies, for example; leadership Luecke (2003) that is identified as very crucial to change management. Therefore, this is an area of study that can investigated further.

This study only focused on the perspective of the RCEP user however there are other stakeholders who have an interest in the project. The perspective of the senior management in the project can be an area that can be investigated to provide a comprehensive analysis into the problematical situation. After all, Keil *et al.* (1998); Kappelman *et al.* (2006) found out in their study that lack of top management support was the main cause of project failure. The competing interests of these perspectives from the different stakeholders will provide a richer and more balanced view of how the problem situation can be improved.

Another area of possible further study is advocated by Leeman (2014) who posits that the existing way of running projects where the project manager is at the helm of the project is flawed and should instead be spearheaded by a change manager is worth investigating further. That the project managers lack the requisite people skills to fully comprehend the requirements and fully manage a project needs further analysis.

Finally, the study was conducted at the United Nations, a global non-profit organization. It is possible that the findings of this research are not necessarily binding in a commercial environment.

5.5 LIMITATIONS

The fear to speak up, by the interviewees, because of victimization fears resulted in the number of participants to the SSM workshop reduced. This also meant that some of the information gathered during the interviews might not be complete and balanced. The lack of familiarity among the SSM participants to SSM meant the researcher was heavily involved in the guiding the participants. To deal with these limitations of the fear to speak up as well as the victimization, the researcher selected to have one-on-one semi-structured interviewees to ensure confidentiality of the participants and also to encourage them to speak up. The reduction of the SSM participants of the workshop avoided a large group which has the potential and risk of only a few dominant participants speaking up. In order to reduce the negative effect of this limitation an environment which allowed participants to freely air out the views was created.

5.6 CONCLUSION

The social side of IT projects is indeed crucial, equally important as the technical side of the project and the project manager needs to have the right balance to ensure one side is not neglected. The study established that the users of IT projects do need to be involved in the project from project initiation and failure to do so can lead to negative perceptions about the project leading to user resistance and ultimately project failure. Communication seen from the lenses of change management is important. It is about ensuring that there is participative environment in how the project is implemented thereby all the stakeholders sharing the vision of the project manager and most importantly claiming part ownership to the project. It is a critical skill that the project manager should have among other skills critical to success like leadership. In a nutshell the study did establish good grounds to assert that the project manager does indeed require to have the change management skill of communication if the project is to avoid failure thereby meeting the objectives and aim of the study.

REFERENCES

Abadie, A., Abbott, A., Abdullah, R., Abma, T., Abravanel, M., Achilles, C., Adams, W.C., Agle, B., Alberti, P. and Allison, G. (2015) Handbook of Practical Program Evaluation, By Kathryn E. Newcomer, Harry P. Hatry and Joseph S. Wholey Copyright© 2015 by Kathryn E. Newcomer, Harry P. Hatry and Joseph S. Wholey. *HANDBOOK OF PRACTICAL PROGRAM EVALUATION*, 833.

Al-Ahmad, W., Al-Fagih, K., Khanfar, K., Alsamara, K., Abuleil, S. and Abu-Salem, H. (2009) A taxonomy of an IT project failure: root causes. *International Management Review*, **5**(1), 93.

Ali, M., Zhou, L., Miller, L. and Ieromonachou, P. (2016) User resistance in IT: A literature review. *International Journal of Information Management*, **36**(1), 35-43.

Anderson, D. and Anderson, L.A. (2010) *Beyond change management: How to achieve breakthrough results through conscious change leadership.* Vol. 36, John Wiley & Sons.

Annonymous (2006) *IT Change Management Still Lacking in Many Organizations.*

Autissier, D. and Moutot, J.-M. (2003) *Pratiques de la conduite du changement: Comment passer du discours à l'action.* Dunod.

Axelrod, D. (1992) Getting everyone involved: How one organization involved its employees, supervisors, and managers in redesigning the organization. *The Journal of applied behavioral science*, **28**(4), 499-509.

Baccarini, D. (1999) The logical framework method for defining project success. *Project Management Journal*, **30**, 25-32.

Bareil, C. and Savoie, A. (1999) Comprendre et mieux gérer les individus en situation de changement organisationnel. *GESTION-MONTREAL-*, **24**, 86-95.

Baskerville, R.L. and Wood-Harper, A.T. (1996) A critical perspective on action research as a method for information systems research. *Journal of information technology*, **11**(3), 235-246.

Behl, A., Gardiner, B. and Finke, J.S. (2016) *Implementing Cisco IP Telephony and Video, Part 1 (CIPTV1) Foundation Learning Guide (CCNP Collaboration Exam 300-070 CIPTV1).* Indianapolis: Cisco Press.

Besson, P. and Rowe, F. (2001) ERP project dynamics and enacted dialogue: perceived understanding, perceived leeway, and the nature of task-related conflicts. *SIGMIS Database*, **32**(4), 47-66.

Beynon-Davies, P. (1995) Information systems 'failure': the case of the London Ambulance Service's Computer Aided Despatch project. *European Journal of Information Systems*, **4**(3), 171-184.

Beynon-Davies, P. (1999) Human error and information systems failure: the case of the London ambulance service computer-aided despatch system project. *Interacting with Computers*, **11**(6), 699-720.

Blaikie, N. (1993) Approaches to Social Enquiry Polity Press. In: Cambridge.

Bokhari, R.H. (2005) The relationship between system usage and user satisfaction: a meta-analysis. *Journal of Enterprise Information Management*, **18**(2), 211-234.

Burrows, D. and Kendall, S. (1997) Focus groups: what are they and how can they be used in nursing and health care research? *Social Sciences in Health*, **3**, 244-253.

Casey, M. and Krueger, R. (1994) Focus group interviewing, *Measurement of food preferences*, pp. 77-96: Springer.

Chang, V., Walters, R.J. and Wills, G. (2013) The development that leads to the Cloud Computing Business Framework. *International Journal of Information Management*, **33**(3), 524-538.

Checkland, P. (1981) *Systems thinking, Systems Practice.* Salisbury: John Wiley & Sons Ltd.

Checkland, P. (2000) Soft systems methodology: a thirty year retrospective. *Systems research and behavioral science*, **17**(S1), S11-S58.

Checkland, P. and Scholes, J. (1990) *Soft systems methodology in action.* Vol. 7, Wiley Chichester.

Checkland, P. and Holwell, S. (1998) *Information, Systems and Information Systems.* John Wiley and Sons.

Checkland, P. and Scholes, J. (1999) *Soft systems methodology: a 30-year retrospective.* John Wiley Chichester.

Checkland, P. and Poulter, J. (2006) *Learning for action.* J. Wiley & Sons.

Checkland, P.B. (1989) Soft systems methodology. *Human systems management*, **8**(4), 273-289.

Cherem, M. (2016) Refugee rights: Against expanding the definition of a "refugee" and unilateral protection elsewhere. *Journal of Political Philosophy*, **24**(2), 183-205.

Cicmil, S. (1999) Implementing organizational change projects: impediments and gaps. *Strategic change*, **8**(2), 119.

Cooke-Davies, T. (2002) The "real" success factors on projects. *International Journal of Project Management*, **20**(3), 185-190.

Cooper, R.G. and Kleinschmidt, E.J. (1987) What makes a new product a winner: Success factors at the project level. *R&D Management*, **17**(3), 175-189.

Crawford, L. and Pollack, J. (2004) Hard and soft projects: a framework for analysis. *International Journal of Project Management*, **22**(8), 645-653.

Crawford, L. and Nahmias, A.H. (2010) Competencies for managing change. *International Journal of Project Management*, **28**(4), 405-412.

Crawford, L., Costello, K., Pollack, J. and Bentley, L. (2003) Managing soft change projects in the public sector. *International Journal of Project Management*, **21**(6), 443-448.

Creasey, T. (2019) PROJECT MANAGEMENT AND CHANGE MANAGEMENT: A SIDE-BY-SIDE COMPARISON. In.

Currie, W. and Galliers, R. (1999) *Rethinking management information systems: An interdisciplinary perspective*. Oxford: Oxford university press.

De Wit, A. (1988) Measurement of project success. *International Journal of Project Management*, **6**(3), 164-170.

Duy Nguyen, L., Ogunlana, S.O. and Thi Xuan Lan, D. (2004) A study on project success factors in large construction projects in Vietnam. *Engineering, Construction and Architectural Management*, **11**(6), 404-413.

Dwivedi, Y.K., Ravichandran, K., Williams, M.D., Miller, S., Lal, B., Antony, G.V. and Kartik, M. (2013) IS/IT project failures: a review of the extant literature for deriving a taxonomy of failure factors. *In, International Working Conference on Transfer and Diffusion of IT*. Springer, 73-88.

Ewusi-Mensah, K. and Przasnyski, Z.H. (1994) Factors contributing to the abandonment of information systems development projects. *Journal of information technology*, **9**(3), 185-201.

Freeman, M. and Beale, P. (1992) Measuring project success. *In*. Project Management Institute.

Gareis, R. (2010) Changes of organizations by projects. *International Journal of Project Management*, **28**(4), 314-327.

Garfein, S.J. and Sankaran, S. (2011) Work Preferences of Project and Program Managers, Change Managers, and Project Team Members: The Importance of Knowing the Difference. In Proceedings of *PMI® Global Congress 2012*, North America, Vancouver, British Columbia, Canada. Newtown Square, PA: Project Management Institute.

Gill, R. (2002) Change management--or change leadership? *Journal of change management*, **3**(4), 307-318.

Gravenhorst, K. and Veld, R. (2004) Power and collaboration: methodologies for working together in change. *Dynamics of organizational change and learning*, 317-341.

Gustavsson, T.K. and Hallin, A. (2014) Rethinking dichotomization: A critical perspective on the use of "hard" and "soft" in project management research. *International Journal of Project Management*, **32**(4), 568-577.

Henrie, M.E. and Sousa-Posa, A. (2005) Project management: A cultural literary review. *In*. Project Management Institute.

Hill, K. (2003) System designs that start at the end (user). *CRM Daily*.

Hirschheim, R. and Newman, M. (1988) Information Systems and User Resistance: Theory and Practice*. *The Computer Journal*, **31**(5), 398-408.

Hornstein, H.A. (2015) The integration of project management and organizational change management is now a necessity. *International Journal of Project Management*, **33**(2), 291-298.

INCOSE (2020) *What is systems engineering* [Online]. San Diego. Available: https://www.incose.org/systems-engineering [Accessed 15/10/2020, 2020].

Jackson, M.C. (2003) *Systems thinking: Creative holism for managers*. Citeseer.

Jacobsen, K.L. and Sandvik, K.B. (2018) UNHCR and the pursuit of international protection: accountability through technology? *Third World Quarterly*, 1-17.

Jain, A. (2004) Using the Lens of Max Weber's Theory of Bureaucracy to Examine E-Government Research. In Proceedings of *Proceedings of the Proceedings of the 37th Annual Hawaii International Conference on System Sciences (HICSS'04) - Track 5 - Volume 5*, 50127.50123.

Jarocki, T.L. (2011) *The Next Evolution-Enhancing and Unifying Project and Change Management: The Emergence One Method for Total Project Success*. San Francisco: Brown & Williams Pub., LLC.

Jasperson, J.S., Carte, T.A., Saunders, C.S., Butler, B.S., Croes, H.J. and Zheng, W. (2002) Power and information technology research: A metatriangulation review. *MIS quarterly*, **26**(4), 397-459.

Jepson, K. (2006) Why One IT Exec emphasizes. *People Dimensions'. 'Credit Union Journal*, **10**(34), 14.

Jiang, J.J., Muhanna, W.A. and Klein, G. (2000) User resistance and strategies for promoting acceptance across system types. *Information & Management*, **37**(1), 25-36.

Joshi, K. (1991) A model of users' perspective on change: the case of information systems technology implementation. *MIS quarterly*, 229-242.

Jurison, J. (2002) Integrating Project Management and Change Management in an IS Curriculum. *Communications of the Association for Information Systems*, **8**(1), 2.

Kanter, R., Stein, B. and Jick, T. (1992) *The challenge of organizational change* New York: The Free Press.

Kappelman, L.A., McKeeman, R. and Zhang, L. (2006) Early warning signs of IT project failure: The dominant dozen. *Information systems management*, **23**(4), 31-36.

Keil, M., Cule, P.E., Lyytinen, K. and Schmidt, R.C. (1998) A framework for identifying software project risks. *Communications of the ACM*, **41**(11), 76-83.

Kerzner, H. and Kerzner, H.R. (2017) *Project management: a systems approach to planning, scheduling, and controlling*. New York: John Wiley & Sons.

Kim, H.-W. and Kankanhalli, A. (2009) Investigating user resistance to information systems implementation: A status quo bias perspective. *MIS quarterly*, 567-582.

Kim, J.U. and Kishore, R. (2018) Do we Fully Understand Information Systems Failure? An Exploratory Study of the Cognitive Schema of IS Professionals. *Information Systems Frontiers*, 1-35.

Klaus, T. and Blanton, J.E. (2010) User resistance determinants and the psychological contract in enterprise system implementations. *European Journal of Information Systems*, **19**(6), 625-636.

Kotter, J.P. (1995) Leading change: Why transformation efforts fail.

Kotter, J.P. (1997) Leading change: why transformation efforts fail. *IEEE Engineering Management Review*, **25**(1), 34-40.

Lapointe, L. and Rivard, S. (2005) A multilevel model of resistance to information technology implementation. *MIS quarterly*, 461-491.

Leeman, R. (2014) Project Management vs Change management. In: *Linkedin*.

Lehmann, V. (2010) Connecting changes to projects using a historical perspective: towards some new canvases for researchers. *International Journal of Project Management*, **28**(4), 328-338.

Lehtinen, T.O., Mäntylä, M.V., Vanhanen, J., Itkonen, J. and Lassenius, C. (2014) Perceived causes of software project failures–An analysis of their relationships. *Information and Software Technology*, **56**(6), 623-643.

Levasseur, R.E. (2010) People skills: Ensuring project success—A change management perspective. *Interfaces*, **40**(2), 159-162.

Levy, A. and Merry, U. (1986) *Organizational transformation: Approaches, strategies, theories*. Greenwood Publishing Group.

Lewin, K. (1947) Change management model. In: New York: McGraw Hill.

Lewin, K. (1951) Field theory in social science.

Lodinová, A. (2016) Application of biometrics as a means of refugee registration: focusing on UNHCR's strategy. *Development, Environment and Foresight*, **2**(2), 91-100.

Luecke, R. (2003) *Managing change and transition*. Vol. 3, Boston, MA: Harvard Business Press.

Lyytinen, K. and Hirschheim, R. (1988) Information systems failures—a survey and classification of the empirical literature. *In, Oxford surveys in information technology*. Oxford University Press, Inc., Vol. 4, 257-309.

Marakas, G.M. and Hornik, S. (1996) Passive resistance misuse: overt support and covert recalcitrance in IS implementation. *European Journal of Information Systems*, **5**(3), 208-219.

Markus, M.L. (1983) Power, politics, and MIS implementation. *Commun. ACM*, **26**(6), 430-444.

Markus, M.L. and Robey, D. (1988) Information technology and organizational change: causal structure in theory and research. *Management science*, **34**(5), 583-598.

Martinko, M.J., Zmud, R.W. and Henry, J.W. (1996) An attributional explanation of individual resistance to the introduction of information technologies in the workplace. *Behaviour & Information Technology*, **15**(5), 313-330.

McConnell, S. (1996) *Rapid development: taming wild software schedules*. Pearson Education.

McManus, J. and Wood-Harper, T. (2007) Understanding the sources of information systems project failure. *Management services*, **51**(3), 38-43.

Moran, J.W. and Brightman, B.K. (2000) Leading organizational change. *Journal of Workplace Learning*, **12**(2), 66-74.

Müller, R. and Turner, J.R. (2007) Matching the project manager's leadership style to project type. *International Journal of Project Management*, **25**(1), 21-32.

Mumford, E. and Weir, M. (1979) *Computer systems in work design--the ETHICS method: effective technical and human implementation of computer systems: a work design exercise book for individuals and groups*. John Wiley & Sons.

Munns, A. and Bjeirmi, B.F. (1996) The role of project management in achieving project success. *International Journal of Project Management*, **14**(2), 81-87.

Nahmias, A.H. (2009) *Who is the Change Manager*. Doctoral book. Department of Sustainable Development, Bond University.

Nawaz, A., Kundi, G.M. and Shah, D. (2007) Metaphorical interpretations of information systems failure. *Peshawar University Teachers' Association Journal*, **14**, 15-26.

Neal, R.A. (1995) Project definition: the soft-systems approach. *International Journal of Project Management*, **13**(1), 5-9.

Nelson, R.R. (2007) IT project management: Infamous failures, classic mistakes, and best practices. *MIS Quarterly executive*, **6**(2).

Nicholas, J.M. and Steyn, H. (2012) *Project management for Engineering, Business and Technology*. Routledge.

OGC: Office of Government Commerce (2009) *Managing successful projects with PRINCE2*. The Stationery Office.

Parker, D., Charlton, J., Ribeiro, A. and D. Pathak, R. (2013) Integration of project-based management and change management: Intervention methodology. *International Journal of Productivity and Performance Management*, **62**(5), 534-544.

Partington, D. (1996) The project management of organizational change. *International Journal of Project Management*, **14**(1), 13-21.

Pinto, J.K. and Slevin, D.P. (1987) Critical factors in successful project implementation. *IEEE transactions on engineering management*(1), 22-27.

PMI (2017) *Success Rates Rise. Transforming the high cost of low performance*. online.

Pollack, J. and Algeo, C. (2014) A comparison of Project Manager and Change Manager involvement in organisational change project activities and stages. *Journal of Modern Project Management*, **2**(2), 8-17.

Pollack, J. and Algeo, C. (2015) The contribution of project management and change management to project success. *The Business & Management Review*, **6**(2), 22.

Project Management Institute (2013) *A guide to the project management body of knowldge: (PMBOK guide), Fifth Edition*. 5th ed. Newton Square, Pa. :Project Management institute.

Ramsay, D.A., Boardman, J.T. and Cole, A.J. (1996) Reinforcing learning, using soft systemic frameworks. *International Journal of Project Management*, **14**(1), 31-36.

Rose, J. (1997) Soft systems methodology as a social science research tool. *Systems Research and Behavioral Science: The Official Journal of the International Federation for Systems Research*, **14**(4), 249-258.

Sandvik, K.B. and Jacobsen, K.L. (2016) *UNHCR and the struggle for accountability: technology, law and results-based management*. Routledge.

Sauer, C. (1993) *Why information systems fail: a case study approach*. Alfred Waller Ltd., Publishers.

Selin, V. (2018) Challenges with UNHCR's RCEP project. In: Chimwe, T., Ed., Pretoria.

Shang, S.S. (2012) Dual strategy for managing user resistance with business integration systems. *Behaviour & Information Technology*, **31**(9), 909-925.

Shenhar, A.J., Dvir, D., Levy, O. and Maltz, A.C. (2001) Project success: a multidimensional strategic concept. *Long range planning*, **34**(6), 699-725.

Silva Alvarado, L.T. (2016) *A Soft Systems Methodology Approach to Multifunctional Landscapes: understanding interactivity and engaging stakeholders*. University of Sheffield.

Simonsen, J. (1994) Soft systems methodology. *An introduction. Roskilde University.. Diakses pada tanggal*, **27**.

Smiles, S. (1904) *Lives of the Engineers George and Robert Stephenson: The Locomotive*. J.M.A. Street.

Standish and Group (2013) *Chaos Report 2013*.

Standish Group (2016) *The Standish Group Report-CHAOS*.

Stewart, R.W. and Fortune, J. (1995) Application of systems thinking to the identification, avoidance and prevention of risk. *International Journal of Project Management*, **13**(5), 279-286.

Stoica, R. and Brouse, P. (2013) IT project failure: A proposed four-phased adaptive multi-method approach. *Procedia Computer Science*, **16**, 728-736.

Sweis, R. (2015) An investigation of failure in information systems projects: The case of Jordan. *Journal of Management Research*, **7**(1), 173-185.

Szczepanik, M. (2016) The'Good'and'Bad'Refugees? Imagined Refugeehood (s) in the Media Coverage of the Migration Crisis. *Journal of Identity and Migration Studies*, **10**(2), 23.

Taherdoost, H. and Keshavarzsaleh, A. (2015) A Theoretical Review on IT Project Success/Failure Factors and Evaluating the Associated Risks. *In, 14th International Conference on Telecommunications and Informatics, Sliema, Malta.*

UNHCR (2016) *2016 Annual Report*.

UNHCR (2018) *Subregion: Southern Africa*. UNHCR.

Urli, B. and Urli, D. (2000) Project management in North America, stability of the concepts. *Project Management Journal*, **31**(3), 33-33.

Venkatesh, V., Morris, M.G., Davis, G.B. and Davis, F.D. (2003) User acceptance of information technology: Toward a unified view. *MIS quarterly*, 425-478.

Waddell, D. and Sohal, A.S. (1998) Resistance: a constructive tool for change management. *Management decision*, **36**(8), 543-548.

Whitney, K.M. and Daniels, C.B. (2013) The root cause of failure in complex IT projects: Complexity itself. *Procedia Computer Science*, **20**, 325-330.

Worsley, L.M. (2017) *Stakeholder-led Project Management - Changing the Way We Manage Projects. Portfoliio and Project Management Collection*, New York: Business Expert Press.

Yeo, K. (1993) Systems thinking and project management—time to reunite. *International Journal of Project Management*, **11**(2), 111-117.

Yeo, K.T. (2002) Critical failure factors in information system projects. *International Journal of Project Management*, **20**(3), 241-246.

Yurtseven, K. (2011) Systems engineering and soft systems methodology: a review. *Doğuş Üniversitesi Dergisi*, **1**(1), 225-230.

Zwikael, O. and Globerson, S. (2006) From critical success factors to critical success processes. *International Journal of Production Research*, **44**(17), 3433-3449.

APPENDIX A - SSM ANALYSIS TWO & THREE: ONE-ON-ONE INTERVIEW SCHEDULE

The next section provides the one-on-one interview schedule for the cultural stream of enquiry, Analysis two (Social System) and Analysis three (Political System). A semi-structured approach was chosen to give the interviewees freedom to express themselves.

A. **Analysis Two (Social System) Questions**

1. General Questions

History:
i. What historical factors are considered important in the organization?
ii. What are some of the prominent figures of the past that are regarded as heroes and why?
iii. Which past stories and important events are continuously retold about the organization both good and bad?
iv. What values are regarded as important and linked to these historical events and figures?
v. How is the IT department regarded historically in the organization? Is it respected?
vi. Which historical IT projects do you remember?
vii. Which of these projects were successful/failures and why?
viii. Were people supportive of IT change projects?
ix. Which methodology was used for the change initiative?
x. Was SSM considered or used?
xi. Was the skill of communication regarded important in past change projects?

Contingency:
i. How are limited resources in the organization distributed and prioritized?
ii. In your view are IT projects given priority?
iii. Do they deserve to be given priority in such situations?
iv. Should the RCEP project be prioritized?
v. Should SSM be used for the RCEP IT change project?

Formalisms
i. What policies within the organization are indispensable?
ii. What structures are historically important in the organization?
iii. How are projects, generally selected in the organization?
iv. How are change projects implemented in the organization?
v. How do you think IT projects should be implemented to you?
vi. Who decides on which projects to undertake?
Vii What is the current Change procedure?

2. ROLES

General Questions
i. What is your role within UNHCR?
ii. How many years have you worked in UNHCR?
iii. How many years of overall experience do you have including outside UNHCR?
iv. Have you worked in another United Nations Agency?
v. Do you have any prior experience in holding roles within change projects?

vi. Do you have any experience holding a project role that requires communication skill?
vii. What role will play to improve the problem situation with the RCEP project?

3. RCEP Related Questions
i. What is your role within the RCEP IT project?
ii. Does your role require you to depend on other roles?
iii. Have you held a similar role before?
iv. How did you perform in that role?
v. Based on your experience what should be added/removed in your view?
Vi Should SSM be used in this project?

4. Norms

i. What is the expected behavior of a UNHCR staff member?
ii. What is the expected behavior within your role in the RCEP project?
iii. Who determines expected behavior in the organization?
iv. Are there any repercussions if you don't abide by expected behavior?
v. What is your personal view about these norms?
vi. Who are the key role models in the organization?
vii. For this project to succeed what should be the expected norm in your view?

5. Values
i. What is regarded as good or bad behavior in the UNHCR?
ii. What is regarded as good or bad behavior in your role within the RCEP project?
iii. What are the conformity expectations?
iv. What are the limits of expected rebellion in the organization?
v. For this project to succeed what should be regarded as good behavior?

B. <u>**Analysis Three (Political System) Questions**</u>

1. Disposition of Power
i. Which department has more power historically?
ii. Which department has more power at the moment?
iii. How much power does the IT department have in the organization?
iv. Which individuals have power currently and historically?
v. Does individual power obtained through Politics, authority or power?
vi. Who has power formal or informal power to influence change in the organization?
vii. Who has the formal power to reject new change projects in the organization?
viii. Does anyone has informal power to be able to influence a new change project?
ix. Are there any cliques in the organization and do they have power?

2. Nature of Power
i. Who has the power to distribute resources in the organization?
ii. Who has the power to influence others to effect change projects?
iii. Does anyone hold the ability to convince others of the need for new change projects?

Process by which power is:
1. **Obtained**:

i. Is power obtained by authority through formal position at UNHCR?
ii. Is power obtained through negotiation where key movers emerge?
iii. Is power obtained through politicking?
iv. Is it obtained by joining cliques?

2. Exercised:
i. Does withholding information gives one power?
ii. Is power exercised based on the formal role one has?
iii. Is power exercised through cliques membership?

3. Preserved:
i. Is power preserved by withholding information?
ii. Does politicking ensure you preserve power?
iii. Is power preserved by joining the right clique?

4. Passed on:
i. Is power passed on through formal means?
ii. Is power passed-on through informal means?
iii. Is power passed on within a clique?